Mastering Drupal 10: Building Powerful and Scalable Websites

Chapter 1: Introduction

Welcome to "Mastering Drupal 10: Building Powerful and Scalable Websites"! In this chapter, we will introduce you to the powerful, flexible, and popular content management system (CMS) called Drupal. This book is designed to help you harness the power of Drupal 10, the latest version of the platform, to create engaging and scalable websites for your business or personal projects.

Drupal has long been a favorite among web developers and site builders due to its extensive functionality and customization options. With an active community contributing to its development and growth, Drupal has become a robust solution for various types of web projects, ranging from personal blogs and small business websites to large enterprise applications and government portals.

In this first chapter, we will explore the key features of Drupal 10, its evolution over the years, and its advantages compared to other content management systems. We will also provide an overview of system requirements and the installation process, setting the stage for more in-depth exploration of Drupal's capabilities in the subsequent chapters.

As you progress through this book, you will gain hands-on experience and practical knowledge of Drupal's powerful features, learning how to create, manage, and optimize your website using the Drupal 10 platform. We will also cover various aspects of Drupal, such as theming, module development, performance optimization, and more, ensuring you have all the tools and knowledge necessary to build a successful Drupal-based website.

So let's begin our journey into the exciting world of Drupal 10 and discover the endless possibilities this exceptional CMS has to offer.

1.1. The Power of Drupal 10

Drupal 10 builds upon the strong foundation of its predecessors, offering new features, improvements, and optimizations that make it more powerful, secure, and user-friendly. As you embark on your Drupal 10 journey, it is essential to understand the key features that set this CMS apart from other content management systems. Here are some of the main advantages of Drupal 10:

Flexibility and Customization

Drupal is known for its modular architecture, which allows you to extend and customize its functionality according to your needs. With thousands of contributed modules available and the ability to create custom modules, you can tailor your Drupal site to suit your specific requirements. The flexible theming system also enables you to create unique designs and layouts for your website.

Scalability and Performance

Drupal's robust architecture and built-in caching mechanisms ensure that your website can handle high traffic loads and grow with your organization. With Drupal 10, performance has been further improved, providing faster page loads and more efficient resource management.

Security

Security is a top priority for Drupal, with a dedicated security team and a strong commitment to addressing potential vulnerabilities. Drupal 10 includes numerous security enhancements, such as more secure password hashing algorithms, improved content filtering, and support for the latest web security standards.

Multilingual and Internationalization

Drupal 10 makes it easier than ever to create multilingual websites. With built-in support for language configuration, content translation, and interface translation, you can deliver a seamless user experience for your global audience.

Integration with Third-Party Services

Drupal's API-first approach and support for web services make it easy to integrate your website with various third-party services, such as social media platforms, CRM systems, and marketing automation tools. This allows you to streamline your workflows and leverage the power of external applications within your Drupal site.

Active Community and Resources

The Drupal community is a vibrant and collaborative group of developers, site builders, and enthusiasts who contribute to the growth and improvement of the platform. This community provides a wealth of resources, such as contributed modules, themes, and documentation, to help you get the most out of Drupal 10.

As you can see, Drupal 10 is a powerful and versatile platform that can accommodate a wide range of web projects. In the following sections, we will dive deeper into the world of Drupal, exploring its history, comparing it with previous versions, and understanding the system requirements and installation process.

1.2. A Brief History of Drupal

Before delving deeper into Drupal 10, let's take a brief look at the history of Drupal and how it has evolved over the years.

Understanding Drupal's development journey will provide you with a better appreciation of its capabilities and the community that supports it.

Origins of Drupal

Drupal was created in 2000 by Dries Buytaert, a Belgian computer science student at the time, as a message board for his university dorm. The project quickly gained traction, and he decided to release it as an open-source platform in 2001, allowing other developers to contribute to its growth. The name "Drupal" is derived from the Dutch word "druppel," which means "drop," symbolizing the platform's origins as a simple message board.

Evolution of Drupal

Since its inception, Drupal has undergone numerous updates and improvements, with each major version release bringing new features and enhancements. Some notable milestones in Drupal's evolution include:

- Drupal 4.7 (2006): Introduced the Forms API and improved support for internationalization, making it easier to build multilingual websites.
- Drupal 5 (2007): Implemented the jQuery JavaScript library, improving the platform's user interface and adding support for AJAX functionality.

- Drupal 6 (2008): Introduced an improved menu system, better performance through CSS and JavaScript optimization, and enhanced security features.
- Drupal 7 (2011): Added the Fields API, allowing developers to add custom fields to any content type, and introduced the Render API for more flexible theming.
- Drupal 8 (2015): Brought a major architectural overhaul with the adoption of Symfony components, the addition of the Twig templating engine, and a focus on "API-first" development. Also introduced significant improvements in multilingual support, configuration management, and the overall user experience.
- Drupal 9 (2020): Streamlined the upgrade process from Drupal 8, removed deprecated code, and updated dependencies to ensure compatibility with the latest web technologies.

Drupal 10: A New Era

With the release of Drupal 10 in 2022, the platform has taken another significant leap forward. Some key features of Drupal 10 include:

- Improved performance and scalability, thanks to the adoption of the latest Symfony and PHP components.
- Enhanced front-end capabilities through the integration of the CKEditor 5 WYSIWYG editor and the new Olivero default theme.

- A stronger focus on accessibility and inclusivity, ensuring that Drupal websites cater to a wide range of users and their unique needs.
- Continued commitment to security and regular updates, making it easier for site owners to maintain a secure and up-to-date website.

As we move forward through this book, we will explore the numerous features and improvements that Drupal 10 has to offer, guiding you through the process of building and maintaining a powerful and scalable Drupal website.

In the next section, we will compare Drupal 10 with previous versions to highlight the key differences and benefits of using the latest release.

1.3. Drupal 10 vs. Previous Versions

As we've seen in the previous section, Drupal has come a long way since its humble beginnings. With each major version release, the platform has introduced new features and improvements to make it more powerful, flexible, and user-friendly. In this section, we'll compare Drupal 10 to previous versions, focusing on the key differences and benefits of using the latest release.

1.3.1. Architectural and Technical Improvements

Drupal 10 builds on the architectural foundation established by Drupal 8 and 9, which saw a significant shift towards a more modern and modular approach. Some of the main architectural and technical improvements in Drupal 10 include:

- Updated Dependencies: Drupal 10 features updated versions of Symfony, PHP, and other dependencies, ensuring compatibility with the latest web technologies and best practices.
- Improved Performance: Thanks to the adoption of the latest Symfony and PHP components, Drupal 10 offers better performance and resource management compared to previous versions.
- Easier Upgrades: The upgrade process between major Drupal versions has been streamlined, making it easier for site owners to keep their websites up-to-date and take advantage of the latest features.

1.3.2. User Experience Enhancements

One of the key focuses of Drupal 10 has been to improve the overall user experience for site builders, content editors, and site visitors. Some notable user experience enhancements in Drupal 10 are:

- New Default Theme - Olivero: Drupal 10 introduces a new, modern, and accessible default theme called Olivero, designed to provide a visually appealing and user-friendly starting point for new websites.

- CKEditor 5 Integration: The new CKEditor 5 WYSIWYG editor provides an improved content editing experience, offering more intuitive controls and better support for media management and embedding.

- Accessibility Improvements: Drupal 10 has a stronger focus on accessibility and inclusivity, ensuring that Drupal websites cater to a wide range of users and their unique needs.

1.3.3. Security and Maintenance

Security has always been a top priority for Drupal, and this commitment continues with Drupal 10. Some of the key security and maintenance features in Drupal 10 include:

- Regular Security Updates: Drupal 10 follows a regular release cycle for security updates, making it easier for site owners to keep their websites secure and protected against potential vulnerabilities.

- Removal of Deprecated Code: By removing deprecated code from previous versions, Drupal 10 ensures a cleaner and more efficient codebase, reducing the likelihood of security issues and making it easier to maintain and extend the platform.

- Improved Password Security: Drupal 10 introduces more secure password hashing algorithms, further enhancing the security of user accounts and protecting sensitive data.

In summary, Drupal 10 builds on the strengths of its predecessors, offering a more powerful, flexible, and user-friendly platform for building and managing websites. By using Drupal 10, you can take advantage of the latest web technologies, best practices, and ongoing community support to create a future-proof website that meets the needs of your organization or project.

In the next section, we will discuss the system requirements for Drupal 10 and provide an overview of the installation process.

1.4. System Requirements and Installation Overview

Before you can begin building your Drupal 10 website, it's essential to understand the system requirements and the installation process. In this section, we will cover the minimum and recommended system requirements for Drupal 10, as well as provide a brief overview of the steps involved in installing Drupal on your server.

1.4.1. System Requirements

To ensure the proper functioning and performance of Drupal 10, your server must meet certain minimum requirements. While it's possible to run Drupal 10 on a server that only meets the minimum requirements, we recommend using a server that exceeds these requirements for better performance and scalability.

Minimum System Requirements

- Web Server: Apache, Nginx, or Microsoft IIS
- Database: MySQL 5.7.8+, MariaDB 10.3.7+, or PostgreSQL 10+
- PHP: Version 8.1 or higher
- Memory: At least 128 MB of PHP memory (256 MB recommended)

Recommended System Requirements

- Web Server: Apache 2.4+ with mod_rewrite enabled or Nginx 1.17+
- Database: MySQL 8.0+, MariaDB 10.5+, or PostgreSQL 12+
- PHP: Version 8.1 or higher
- Memory: 256 MB or more of PHP memory
- Additional PHP Extensions: php-gd, php-curl, php-dom, and php-mbstring

Note that these requirements are subject to change, and it's always a good idea to consult the official Drupal documentation for the most up-to-date information on system requirements.

1.4.2. Installation Overview

Installing Drupal 10 involves several steps, which can vary depending on your server environment and preferences. The following is a general overview of the installation process:

1. Download and Extract Drupal: Download the latest Drupal 10 release from the official Drupal website and extract the files to your local computer.

2. Upload Files to Your Server: Upload the extracted Drupal files to your web server, either in the root directory or a subdirectory, depending on your desired site structure.

3. Create a Database: Using your server's database management system (e.g., phpMyAdmin, MySQL command line, etc.), create a new database and user for your Drupal installation.

4. Configure Your Web Server: Ensure your web server is configured correctly to serve the Drupal files and handle URL rewriting (if using clean URLs).

5. Run the Drupal Installer: Navigate to your Drupal site's URL in your web browser, which should automatically initiate the Drupal installer. Follow the on-screen prompts to configure your site settings, database connection, and initial site administrator account.

6. Install and Configure Modules and Themes: Once the core installation is complete, you can begin installing and configuring additional modules and themes to extend the functionality and appearance of your site.

In the subsequent chapters of this book, we will guide you through each of these steps in greater detail, ensuring that you have a solid understanding of the Drupal installation process and can effectively set up your Drupal 10 website.

With the foundation laid, we will now move on to explore the various aspects of Drupal 10, starting with its architecture and key components in the next chapter.

1.4.3. Installing Drupal using Composer

Composer is a dependency management tool for PHP that simplifies the process of managing and installing packages, including Drupal and its modules and themes. Here's an overview of how to install Drupal 10 using Composer:

1. Install Composer: If you haven't already, install Composer on your local machine or server. You can find the installation instructions for your operating system on the official Composer website: https://getcomposer.org/

2. Create a New Drupal Project: In your command line interface, navigate to the directory where you want to install Drupal, and run the following command to create a new Drupal project using Composer:

```
composer create-project drupal/recommended-project my_site_name_dir
```

Replace my_site_name_dir with the desired directory name for your Drupal installation.

This command will download and install the latest version of Drupal along with its required dependencies.

3. Configure Web Server: Make sure your web server is properly configured to serve the Drupal files and handle URL rewriting (if using clean URLs). Point your web server's document root to the web directory within the Drupal project folder.

4. Create a Database: Using your server's database management system (e.g., phpMyAdmin, MySQL command line, etc.), create a new database and user for your Drupal installation.

5. Run the Drupal Installer: Follow steps 5 and 6 from the Installation Overview (1.4.2) to complete the Drupal installation using the web-based installer.

Using Composer for your Drupal installation is a recommended approach as it simplifies the management of modules, themes, and dependencies. Furthermore, it allows you to easily keep your

Drupal installation up-to-date by running simple Composer commands.

Chapter 2: Getting Started with Drupal 10

In this chapter, we will guide you through the initial steps to help you familiarize yourself with Drupal 10 and start building your website. We will cover various essential aspects, such as navigating the administrative interface, managing content, configuring site settings, working with user accounts and permissions, and understanding the basics of themes and modules. By the end of this chapter, you will have a strong foundation to build upon as you continue to explore and utilize Drupal 10's powerful features.

First, let's discuss the Drupal administrative interface, which is where you will spend most of your time managing and configuring your website. The administrative interface, also known as the backend, is designed to be user-friendly and intuitive. Upon logging in as an administrator, you will be greeted with a toolbar at the top of the screen that provides access to various site management sections, such as content, structure, appearance, and configuration.

In the content section, you can create, edit, and manage various types of content, including articles, basic pages, and custom content types you have defined. This section also allows you to manage media assets, such as images and documents, and organize your content using categories and tags.

The structure section is where you can define and manage the overall structure of your website, including content types, menus, views, and blocks. You can create custom content types with unique fields and display settings, define menu hierarchies for easy site navigation, build dynamic views to display lists of content, and manage blocks that provide additional functionality and content to various regions of your site's layout.

In the appearance section, you can manage your site's themes, which control the visual presentation and layout of your website. You can install and enable new themes, customize existing themes, and define various settings related to your site's appearance.

The configuration section allows you to manage various site-wide settings, such as the site name, slogan, timezone, and email address for system notifications. You can also configure settings related to content authoring, media handling, search functionality, and more.

Another essential aspect of managing a Drupal website is working with user accounts and permissions. In Drupal 10, you can create and manage user accounts, define roles with specific permissions, and control access to various features and functionalities based on user roles. This system allows you to maintain a secure and organized website by granting users access only to the features and sections they need.

Finally, we will touch upon the basics of modules and themes in Drupal 10. As mentioned earlier, modules are individual components that extend the functionality of your website, while themes control its visual appearance and layout. Drupal's modular architecture enables you to easily customize and extend your site by installing and configuring a wide variety of contributed and custom modules and themes.

In the following chapters, we will delve deeper into each of these areas, providing detailed explanations, examples, and best practices to help you effectively build and manage your Drupal 10 website.

2.1. Navigating the Administrative Interface

After successfully installing Drupal 10, you will have access to the administrative interface, where you can manage and configure your website. The administrative interface, also known as the backend, provides an organized and user-friendly environment for website management.

2.1.1. Toolbar

When logged in as an administrator, you will see a toolbar at the top of the screen. This toolbar provides quick access to various sections of the administrative interface, such as Content, Structure, Appearance, Extend, Configuration, People, Reports, and Help.

- Content: This section allows you to create, edit, and manage different types of content on your site, such as articles and basic pages. You can also manage media assets, like images and documents, and organize content using taxonomy terms and vocabularies.

- Structure: Here, you can manage the overall structure of your site, including content types, menus, views, and blocks. You can create custom content types with unique fields and display settings, define menu hierarchies, build dynamic views to display lists of content, and manage blocks that provide additional functionality and content to various regions of your site's layout.

- Appearance: In this section, you can manage your site's themes, which control the visual presentation and layout. You can install and enable new themes, customize existing themes, and define various settings related to your site's appearance.

- Extend: This is where you can manage your site's modules, enabling or disabling them as needed. Modules are individual components that extend the functionality of your website.

- Configuration: The Configuration section allows you to manage various site-wide settings, such as the site name, slogan, timezone, and email address for system notifications. You can also configure settings related to content authoring, media handling, search functionality, and more.

- People: This section is dedicated to managing user accounts, roles, and permissions. You can create new user accounts, define roles with specific permissions, and control access to various features and sections of your site based on user roles.

- Reports: In the Reports section, you can access various logs and reports that provide insights into the activity and performance of your site. Some examples include the recent log messages, available updates, and the status report.
- Help: The Help section provides documentation and support resources for Drupal 10, including explanations of various features, modules, and themes.

2.1.2. Dashboard

In addition to the toolbar, Drupal 10 offers a customizable dashboard that provides an overview of your site's content, user activity, and system updates. You can access the dashboard by clicking the "Dashboard" link in the toolbar or by visiting /admin/dashboard in your browser.

By default, the dashboard contains several blocks, such as "Recent content," "Who's online," and "Recent log messages." However, you can customize the dashboard to include additional blocks or rearrange the existing blocks to suit your needs.

By understanding and utilizing the administrative interface effectively, you can efficiently manage and configure your Drupal 10 website. In the following sections, we will explore various aspects of Drupal 10 in more detail, starting with content management.

2.2. Content Management in Drupal 10

Creating, editing, and managing content is at the core of any website, and Drupal 10 provides a powerful and flexible content management system (CMS) to help you efficiently manage your site's content. In this section, we will explore the basics of content management in Drupal, including content types, creating and editing content, and organizing content using taxonomy.

2.2.1. Content Types

Drupal 10 comes with two built-in content types: Article and Basic Page. An Article is typically used for time-sensitive content, such as news updates or blog posts, while a Basic Page is used for static content that doesn't change often, such as an "About Us" or "Contact" page.

You can also create custom content types to suit your specific needs. Custom content types can have their own unique fields, display settings, and other configurations. Creating custom content types allows you to structure and organize your content more effectively, making it easier for both site administrators and visitors to find and interact with the content.

2.2.2. Creating and Editing Content

To create new content, navigate to the "Content" section in the administrative toolbar and click on the "Add content" button. You will be presented with a list of available content types. Select the desired content type and fill in the required fields, such as the title, body, and any additional custom fields you have defined for that content type.

Drupal provides a user-friendly editor for creating and editing content. The editor includes various formatting options, such as bold, italic, lists, and links, as well as the ability to add images and other media assets. You can also manage the URL alias, meta tags, and other SEO-related settings for each piece of content.

When editing content, you can save your changes as a draft or publish them immediately. Drupal also offers a revision system that allows you to track changes and revert to previous versions if necessary.

2.2.3. Organizing Content with Taxonomy

Drupal's taxonomy system enables you to organize and categorize your content using terms and vocabularies. A vocabulary is a collection of related terms, and each term can be assigned to one or more pieces of content. Using taxonomy helps you create a more organized and user-friendly site, making it easier for visitors to find and navigate related content.

By default, Drupal comes with a "Tags" vocabulary that can be used to categorize content using free-form tags. You can also create your own custom vocabularies and terms to better suit your site's structure and organization.

To manage your site's taxonomy, navigate to the "Structure" section in the administrative toolbar and click on the "Taxonomy" link. From here, you can add, edit, and delete vocabularies and terms, as well as configure their settings and hierarchy.

Understanding and utilizing Drupal's content management features will help you efficiently create, edit, and organize content on your website. In the following sections, we will explore other essential aspects of Drupal 10, such as site structure, user management, and modules and themes.

2.3. Managing Users and Permissions

In Drupal 10, managing user accounts and permissions is essential for maintaining a secure and organized website. As an administrator, you can create and manage user accounts, define roles with specific permissions, and control access to various features and sections of your site based on user roles.

2.3.1. User Accounts

To create a new user account, navigate to the "People" section in the administrative toolbar and click on the "Add user" button.

From here, you can specify the user's username, email address, password, and other optional fields.

You can also manage existing user accounts from the "People" section. For example, you can edit user account details, reset passwords, and delete user accounts as needed.

2.3.2. User Roles and Permissions

Drupal 10's role-based permissions system allows you to define specific permissions for different types of users on your site. You can create and manage roles, which are collections of permissions, and assign users to these roles as needed.

By default, Drupal comes with several predefined roles, including Anonymous user, Authenticated user, and Administrator. Anonymous users are visitors who are not logged in to your site, while authenticated users are visitors who have created an account and are logged in. Administrators have full access to all site features and settings.

You can create custom roles to suit your specific needs, such as "Content Editor" or "Moderator." You can then assign specific permissions to each role, such as the ability to create or edit content, manage user accounts, or access specific sections of the site.

2.3.3. User Permissions

Drupal 10 provides a granular permissions system that allows you to control access to various features and sections of your site based on user roles. You can define permissions for each role, such as the ability to create or edit content, access specific administrative features, or view certain types of content.

To manage permissions, navigate to the "People" section in the administrative toolbar and click on the "Permissions" link. From here, you can assign permissions to each role and configure the specific settings for each permission.

By effectively managing user accounts and permissions in Drupal 10, you can maintain a secure and organized website that provides a smooth and tailored user experience.

2.4. Configuring Basic Site Settings

After installing Drupal 10, there are several basic settings you should configure to ensure your site runs smoothly and efficiently. In this section, we will cover some of the essential site settings, including site name, timezone, email address, and search functionality.

2.4.1. Site Name and Slogan

Your site name and slogan appear in various places on your site, such as the browser title bar and the header region. To configure your site name and slogan, navigate to the "Configuration" section in the administrative toolbar and click on the "Site information" link. From here, you can enter your site name and slogan, as well as configure other related settings, such as the site's default front page and logo.

2.4.2. Timezone

Configuring the correct timezone for your site is essential for accurate date and time display and scheduling functionality. To set the timezone for your site, navigate to the "Configuration" section in the administrative toolbar and click on the "Regional and language" link. From here, you can select the appropriate timezone from the list of available options.

2.4.3. Email Address

Drupal 10 uses the site's email address for various system notifications, such as user registration and password reset emails. To configure the site's email address, navigate to the "Configuration" section in the administrative toolbar and click on the "System" link. From here, you can enter the site's email address and configure related settings, such as the "From" name and email address.

2.4.4. Search Functionality

Drupal 10 comes with powerful built-in search functionality that allows visitors to search for content on your site. To configure search settings, navigate to the "Configuration" section in the administrative toolbar and click on the "Search and metadata" link. From here, you can configure settings such as the search index, search fields, and search page settings.

By configuring these basic site settings in Drupal 10, you can ensure that your site runs smoothly and efficiently and provides a user-friendly experience for visitors. In the following sections, we will explore other essential aspects of Drupal 10, such as modules and themes, customizing your site's appearance, and optimizing performance.

Chapter 3: Content Management

Creating and managing content is at the heart of any successful website, and Drupal 10 provides a powerful and flexible content management system (CMS) to help you do just that. In this chapter, we will explore the various tools and features Drupal 10 offers for content management, including content types, fields, views, and media management.

3.1. Content Types and Fields

As mentioned earlier, content types and fields are the foundation of Drupal's content management system, allowing you to define the structure and fields for different types of content on your site. In this section, we will explore how to create and manage content types and fields in Drupal 10.

3.1.1. Creating Content Types

To create a new content type, navigate to the "Structure" section in the administrative toolbar and click on the "Content types" link. From here, you can select the "Add content type" button and specify the name and description for the new content type.

You can then add fields to the new content type by clicking on the "Manage fields" tab. From here, you can add new fields or reuse existing fields, specifying the data type and field settings for each field.

3.1.2. Managing Fields

To manage fields in Drupal 10, navigate to the "Structure" section in the administrative toolbar and click on the "Content types" link. From here, select the content type you wish to manage and click on the "Manage fields" tab.

You can then add new fields, delete existing fields, or edit the settings for each field. You can also change the display settings for each field, such as label and formatting options.

3.1.3. Reusing Fields

In Drupal 10, you can reuse existing fields across multiple content types, making it easier to manage and maintain your content. To reuse a field, navigate to the "Manage fields" tab for the content type you wish to add the field to and select the "Add existing field" button. From here, you can select the field you wish to reuse and configure its settings for the current content type.

By effectively managing content types and fields in Drupal 10, you can create a structured and organized content management system that makes it easy to manage and display your site's content.

3.1.4. Managing Field Widgets

To manage field widgets in Drupal 10, navigate to the "Structure" section in the administrative toolbar and click on the "Content types" link. From here, select the content type you wish to manage and click on the "Manage form display" or "Manage display" tab.

The "Manage form display" tab controls the input widgets for the fields, while the "Manage display" tab controls the display widgets for the fields. You can add, remove, or rearrange widgets for each field, specifying the settings and options for each widget.

For example, you can choose to display a text field as a select list or a radio button, or display an image field as a thumbnail or a full-size image.

By managing field widgets effectively, you can create a user-friendly and intuitive content management system that makes it easy to input and display data on your site.

3.2. Taxonomy: Organizing Your Content

In Drupal 10, taxonomy is a powerful tool for organizing and categorizing content on your site. Taxonomy allows you to create vocabularies, which are collections of related terms, and apply them to content, creating a hierarchical organization that makes it easy to find and manage your site's content.

3.2.1. Creating Vocabularies

To create a new vocabulary, navigate to the "Structure" section in the administrative toolbar and click on the "Taxonomy" link. From here, you can select the "Add vocabulary" button and specify the name and description for the new vocabulary.

You can then add terms to the new vocabulary by clicking on the "Add term" button. From here, you can specify the name and description for each term, as well as the parent term, if applicable.

3.2.2. Applying Taxonomy to Content

Once you have created a vocabulary and added terms, you can apply the vocabulary to content types on your site. To do this, navigate to the "Structure" section in the administrative toolbar and click on the "Content types" link. From here, select the content type you wish to apply the vocabulary to and click on the "Manage fields" tab.

You can then add a new field to the content type, selecting the "Term reference" data type. From here, you can select the vocabulary you wish to use and configure other settings, such as whether to allow multiple terms or whether to display the terms as checkboxes or a select list.

3.2.3. Managing Taxonomy

To manage taxonomy in Drupal 10, navigate to the "Structure" section in the administrative toolbar and click on the "Taxonomy" link. From here, you can select the vocabulary you wish to manage and edit the terms as needed. You can also configure settings for each vocabulary, such as the permissions for adding and editing terms.

By effectively using taxonomy in Drupal 10, you can create a well-organized and easy-to-navigate site that provides a smooth user experience and makes it easy to manage and find content.

3.3. Creating and Editing Content

In Drupal 10, creating and editing content is a simple and intuitive process that allows you to quickly and easily add or update content on your site. In this section, we will explore the steps involved in creating and editing content in Drupal 10.

3.3.1. Creating Content

To create a new piece of content in Drupal 10, navigate to the "Content" section in the administrative toolbar and click on the "Add content" button. From here, you can select the content type you wish to create and fill out the fields for the new content.

You can also apply taxonomy terms to the content by selecting them from the relevant vocabulary, as discussed in the previous section.

3.3.2. Editing Content

To edit existing content in Drupal 10, navigate to the "Content" section in the administrative toolbar and select the piece of content you wish to edit. From here, you can click on the "Edit" button and make changes to the content as needed.

You can also add or remove taxonomy terms from the content by selecting or deselecting them from the relevant vocabulary.

3.3.3. Editing Content with Quick Edit

To use Quick Edit in Drupal 10, you must first enable it for the content types you wish to use it on. To do this, navigate to the "Structure" section in the administrative toolbar and click on the "Content types" link. From here, select the content type you wish to enable Quick Edit for and click on the "Manage display" tab.

From here, you can select the fields you wish to make editable with Quick Edit by checking the "Enable Quick Edit" box next to each field. You can also choose to enable Quick Edit for the entire content row by checking the "Enable Quick Edit" box next to the "Content" field.

Once you have enabled Quick Edit for your desired fields, you can access it by navigating to the front-end of your site and hovering over the content you wish to edit. From here, you can click on the Quick Edit icon to open a pop-up window that allows you to make changes to the content.

Quick Edit in Drupal 10 is a powerful and efficient tool for making quick updates to content on your site, without the need to navigate to the back-end administrative area. By using Quick Edit, you can save time and streamline your content management workflow.

3.3.4. Revisions

Drupal 10 provides a built-in revisions system that allows you to track changes made to content over time. When you make changes to a piece of content, a new revision is created, which can be viewed and compared to previous revisions.

To view and manage revisions for a piece of content, navigate to the "Content" section in the administrative toolbar and select the piece of content you wish to manage. From here, you can click on the "Revisions" tab and view all previous revisions for the content.

By utilizing Drupal 10's content creation and editing features, you can easily manage and update content on your site, ensuring that it stays current and relevant for your audience.

3.3.5. Workflows and Content Moderation

Workflows and content moderation in Drupal 10 provide a powerful set of tools for managing the content creation and publishing process on your site. Workflows allow you to define the steps involved in creating and publishing content, as well as the roles and permissions required for each step. For example, you can define a workflow where content editors create draft content, which is then reviewed by an approver, and finally published by an administrator.

Content moderation in Drupal 10 allows you to manage the editorial process for your site's content, giving you the ability to review and approve content changes before they are published. You can also configure settings for each content type, such as whether changes require approval or whether they can be published immediately.

By effectively utilizing Drupal 10's content editing features, including Quick Edit, revisions, workflows, and content moderation, you can create a well-managed and up-to-date website that effectively showcases your content and provides a smooth user experience.

3.4. Managing Media: Images, Videos, and Files

One of the essential components of a website is media, such as images, videos, and files. Drupal 10 provides powerful tools for managing media on your website, allowing you to easily upload, organize, and display media on your site.

3.4.1. Media Library

Drupal 10's Media Library provides a centralized location for managing all the media assets used on your site. From the Media Library, you can upload new media, organize existing media into folders, and manage the metadata associated with each piece of media.

The Media Library also provides a range of tools for managing media, including bulk uploads, drag and drop reordering, and previews of media assets.

3.4.2. Image Management

Images are a crucial component of many websites, and Drupal 10 provides a range of tools for managing images on your site. You can upload images directly from the Media Library, and Drupal 10 provides a range of image editing tools, such as cropping and resizing, to help you optimize your images for your site.

Drupal 10 also provides a range of options for displaying images on your site, including image galleries, slideshows, and lightboxes.

3.4.2.1. Image Styles

In addition to the basic image editing tools, Drupal 10 also provides a powerful image processing system called Image Styles. Image Styles allow you to create custom versions of images on your site that are optimized for specific display contexts, such as thumbnails, teasers, or full-sized images.

With Image Styles, you can set the size and dimensions of each image, as well as other properties such as image quality, compression, and file format. You can also apply filters to images, such as brightness and contrast adjustments or image effects like rounded corners or drop shadows.

One of the primary benefits of Image Styles is that they allow you to reduce the file size of images on your site, improving site performance and reducing page load times. By creating smaller, optimized versions of images, you can provide users with a fast and engaging browsing experience, even on slower connections or older devices.

Overall, Image Styles provide a powerful tool for managing images on your site, allowing you to create custom versions of images that are optimized for specific display contexts, improving site performance and providing a better user experience.

3.4.2.2. Setting Up Image Styles

One of the powerful features of Drupal 10's image management system is the ability to create custom image styles. Image styles allow you to create optimized versions of images for specific display contexts, such as thumbnails or teasers. Here's how to set up an image style in Drupal 10:

1. First, navigate to the "Image styles" page by going to "Configuration" > "Media" > "Image styles".
2. Click on the "Add image style" button to create a new image style.
3. Give your image style a name that describes the purpose of the style, such as "Thumbnail" or "Teaser".
4. Under the "Effects" section, you can add any image effects that you want to apply to the images. For example, you can add a "Crop" effect to ensure that the image is cropped to the correct aspect ratio for your site.
5. You can also adjust the "Width" and "Height" fields to set the maximum dimensions for the image. This will ensure that the image is resized to fit within these dimensions while maintaining its aspect ratio.
6. Once you have set up the image style, you can use it to display images on your site by referencing it in your image fields. To do this, edit the field settings for the image field and select the appropriate image style from the "Display settings" section.

Setting up image styles in Drupal 10 is an essential step in creating a visually engaging website. By creating custom versions of images that are optimized for specific display contexts, you can improve site performance and provide a better user experience for your site's visitors.

3.4.3. Video Management

Video is another important component of many websites, and Drupal 10 provides tools for managing and displaying video on your site. You can upload videos directly to the Media Library and use Drupal 10's built-in video player to display them on your site.

In addition to the built-in video player, Drupal 10 also supports integration with third-party video platforms, such as YouTube and Vimeo, allowing you to embed videos from these platforms directly on your site.

3.4.4. File Management

Finally, Drupal 10 provides tools for managing files on your site, such as PDFs, Word documents, and other file types. You can upload files directly to the Media Library and manage the metadata associated with each file.

Overall, Drupal 10's media management tools provide a powerful set of features for managing media on your site. Whether you need to upload images, videos, or files, Drupal 10 makes it easy to organize and display your media, ensuring that your site's content is engaging and visually appealing.

Chapter 4: Layout and Theming

Layout and theming are essential components of any Drupal 10 site. They determine the look and feel of your site, as well as how content is organized and displayed.

In Drupal 10, you can use a range of tools and techniques to create custom layouts for your site's content. One of the primary tools for creating layouts is the Layout Builder, a drag-and-drop interface that allows you to create complex layouts for your site's content without the need for coding.

The Layout Builder provides a range of features that allow you to customize the layout of your site's content. For example, you can add and configure sections, columns, and blocks to create custom layouts for different types of content. You can also adjust the spacing and alignment of elements, change the background color or image, and add custom CSS classes to style the layout as needed.

In addition to the Layout Builder, Drupal 10 provides a range of other layout tools and techniques, such as custom templates and themes, that allow you to create unique layouts for your site's content. You can create custom templates for specific content types, such as blog posts or product pages, and use themes to apply consistent styling and branding across your site.

Theming is another essential component of Drupal 10 that allows you to customize the look and feel of your site. Drupal 10 provides a powerful theming system that allows you to create custom themes, modify existing themes, and apply different themes to different parts of your site.

To create a custom theme, you can start with an existing base theme or create a new theme from scratch. Drupal 10's theming system provides a range of tools and techniques, such as template files and CSS stylesheets, that allow you to customize the appearance of your site's content.

Overall, layout and theming are essential components of any Drupal 10 site. By using the Layout Builder, custom templates, and themes, you can create unique and engaging layouts for your site's content and apply consistent branding and styling across your site.

4.1. Understanding Drupal's Theme System

Drupal's theming system is one of the most powerful features of the platform. Understanding how the theme system works is essential for customizing the appearance of your site and creating custom themes.

At its core, Drupal's theme system is built around templates. Templates are PHP files that define the structure and layout of a specific part of your site's content. For example, there are templates for nodes, pages, and blocks.

Drupal's theme system also uses theme functions to generate HTML output. Theme functions are PHP functions that generate HTML output for a specific element of your site's content. For example, there are theme functions for generating links, buttons, and images.

To customize the appearance of your site, you can create custom templates and theme functions. By creating custom templates and functions, you can override the default output and define your own HTML structure and styling.

In addition to templates and theme functions, Drupal's theme system also provides a range of other tools and techniques, such as CSS stylesheets and JavaScript files, that allow you to customize the appearance and behavior of your site's content.

Overall, understanding Drupal's theme system is essential for customizing the appearance of your site and creating custom themes. By mastering the tools and techniques provided by Drupal's theme system, you can create unique and engaging layouts for your site's content and apply consistent branding and styling across your site.

4.2. Working with Layouts and Blocks

In Drupal 10, you can use layouts and blocks to create custom page layouts and organize your site's content. Layouts provide a structure for your pages, while blocks allow you to add and arrange content within those structures.

To work with layouts in Drupal 10, you can use the Layout Builder. The Layout Builder provides a drag-and-drop interface that allows you to create custom layouts for your pages without the need for coding. You can add and arrange sections and columns, as well as adjust the spacing and alignment of elements.

Blocks, on the other hand, are individual pieces of content that can be added to your pages. Blocks can contain anything from text and images to forms and menus. In Drupal 10, you can use the Block Layout page to add and arrange blocks within your page layout. You can also create custom blocks using the Block Content type.

By working with layouts and blocks in Drupal 10, you can create custom page layouts and organize your site's content in a way that makes sense for your users. With the Layout Builder and Block Layout pages, you have powerful tools at your disposal to create engaging and effective page layouts for your Drupal 10 site.

4.3. Customizing Themes

Theming is an essential component of any Drupal 10 site, as it allows you to customize the appearance of your site and create a unique visual identity. Drupal 10's theming system is based on a combination of templates, theme functions, and CSS stylesheets.

To get started with theming in Drupal 10, you can create a custom theme or modify an existing theme. Drupal 10 provides a range of base themes that you can use as a starting point for your custom theme, or you can create a new theme from scratch.

Once you have created a custom theme, you can begin modifying the appearance of your site by editing the theme's templates and CSS stylesheets. Templates allow you to control the structure and layout of your site's content, while CSS stylesheets allow you to modify the appearance of your site's elements, such as fonts, colors, and backgrounds.

In addition to templates and CSS stylesheets, Drupal 10's theming system also provides a range of theme functions that allow you to customize the output of specific elements on your site. For example, you can use theme functions to customize the output of links, buttons, and images.

By mastering Drupal 10's theming system, you can create custom themes that reflect your site's unique visual identity and provide a better user experience for your site's visitors. With a little bit of coding knowledge and creativity, you can create visually stunning and engaging Drupal 10 sites that stand out from the crowd.

4.4. Responsive Design and Accessibility

Twig is a template engine used by Drupal 10's theming system to generate HTML output. Twig provides a powerful and flexible system for creating and modifying templates, allowing you to customize the appearance of your site's content in a way that is both easy to understand and maintainable.

To work with Twig templates in Drupal 10, you first need to understand how they are structured. Twig templates are made up of a series of blocks, which are defined by tags and functions. These blocks can be customized and overridden in your custom theme to modify the output of specific elements on your site.

Twig templates also allow you to use variables to dynamically generate content based on your site's data. For example, you can use variables to display the title of a page, the name of a user, or the contents of a field.

To modify an existing Twig template in Drupal 10, you can create a new template file in your custom theme and use the correct naming convention to target the specific template you want to modify. You can then override specific blocks or add new blocks to customize the output of the template.

Overall, working with Twig templates in Drupal 10 provides a powerful and flexible way to customize the appearance of your site's content. With a little bit of knowledge of Twig's syntax and structure, you can create visually stunning and engaging Drupal 10 sites that meet the specific needs of your site's users.

4.5. Creating Custom Themes and Templates

Creating custom themes and templates is a great way to customize the appearance of your Drupal 10 site and make it stand out from the crowd. While there are many base themes and pre-made templates available for Drupal 10, creating your own custom theme allows you to have complete control over the look and feel of your site.

To create a custom theme in Drupal 10, you first need to decide on a base theme to use as a starting point. Drupal 10 provides several base themes, such as Stable and Classy, that you can use as a starting point for your custom theme.

Once you have selected a base theme, you can create a new directory in your Drupal 10 site's themes directory and give it a unique name. Inside this directory, you can create a series of files and subdirectories to define the structure and appearance of your custom theme.

The primary file for defining the structure of your custom theme is the theme.info.yml file. This file contains information about your theme, such as its name, description, and version, as well as any dependencies it may have.

To define the appearance of your custom theme, you can create a series of Twig templates in the templates subdirectory of your custom theme directory. These templates define the HTML structure and appearance of your site's content, and can be customized to meet your specific needs.

In addition to the theme.info.yml and Twig templates, you can also include CSS stylesheets and JavaScript files in your custom theme directory to modify the appearance and behavior of your site's elements.

By creating a custom theme in Drupal 10, you can have complete control over the appearance of your site and create a unique visual identity that sets your site apart from others. While creating a custom theme does require some coding knowledge and experience, the flexibility and control it provides make it a powerful tool for creating visually stunning and engaging Drupal 10 sites.

4.5.1. Creating Twig Templates for Your Custom Theme

Twig is a powerful templating engine used by Drupal 10 to generate HTML output. To create a custom theme in Drupal 10, you will need to create custom Twig templates that define the HTML structure and appearance of your site's content.

To get started with creating Twig templates for your custom theme, you first need to understand the basics of Twig syntax. Twig uses a series of tags and functions to define the structure of your templates and generate output based on your site's data.

One of the most important tags in Twig is the {{ }} tag, which is used to output variables in your templates. For example, if you want to display the title of a node in your template, you can use the {{ node.title }} syntax to output the title variable.

Twig templates also allow you to use control structures, such as loops and conditionals, to generate dynamic content based on your site's data. For example, you can use a for loop to output a list of items, or an if statement to conditionally output content based on certain criteria.

To create a new Twig template for your custom theme, you can create a new file in the templates subdirectory of your custom theme directory and give it a unique name. You can then use Twig's syntax to define the structure and appearance of your template.

In addition to creating new Twig templates, you can also override existing templates in your custom theme. To do this, you can create a new Twig template with the same name as the template you want to override in your custom theme directory. Drupal 10 will automatically use your custom template instead of the default template.

Overall, creating custom Twig templates is an essential part of creating a custom theme in Drupal 10. By mastering Twig's syntax and structure, you can create visually stunning and engaging templates that meet the specific needs of your site's users. With a little bit of coding knowledge and creativity, you can create custom templates that set your site apart from others and provide a better user experience for your site's visitors.

4.5.2. Popular Twig Syntax

Twig is a powerful and flexible templating engine that provides a range of syntax options for creating custom templates for your Drupal 10 site. Here are some popular Twig syntax options that you might find useful:

- Output variables: You can output variables in your templates using the {{ }} syntax. For example, to output the title of a node, you can use {{ node.title }}.
- Control structures: Twig provides a range of control structures that allow you to generate dynamic content based on your site's data. For example, you can use a for loop to output a list of items, or an if statement to conditionally output content based on certain criteria.
- Filters: Filters allow you to modify the output of variables in your templates. Here are some popular Twig filters:
    - trim: The trim filter removes whitespace from the beginning and end of a string. For example, to remove whitespace from a variable called

my_string, you can use the following syntax: {{ my_string|trim }}

- length: The length filter returns the length of a string or array. For example, to get the length of a variable called my_array, you can use the following syntax: {{ my_array|length }}
- upper and lower: The upper and lower filters convert a string to uppercase or lowercase, respectively. For example, to convert a variable called my_string to uppercase, you can use the following syntax: {{ my_string|upper }}
- date: The date filter formats a date variable in a specific way. For example, to format a date variable called my_date as "January 1, 2023", you can use the following syntax: {{ my_date|date("F j, Y") }}
- replace: The replace filter replaces all occurrences of a substring with another string. For example, to replace all occurrences of "hello" with "hi" in a variable called my_string, you can use the following syntax: {{ my_string|replace("hello", "hi") }}
- default: The default filter returns a default value if a variable is undefined or null. For example, to set a default value of "N/A" for a variable called my_variable, you can use the following syntax: {{ my_variable|default("N/A") }}
- Functions: Functions provide additional functionality for your templates beyond what is built into Twig. For

example, you can use the path function to generate a URL for a specific page on your site.

- Macros: Macros allow you to define reusable chunks of code that can be used throughout your templates. For example, you can create a macro for displaying a social media icon that can be used on multiple pages.
- Includes: Includes allow you to reuse parts of your templates across multiple pages. For example, you can create a header include that can be used on every page of your site.

By mastering these popular Twig syntax options, you can create custom templates for your Drupal 10 site that provide a better user experience and meet the specific needs of your site's visitors. With a little bit of coding knowledge and creativity, you can create visually stunning and engaging templates that set your site apart from others.

4.5.3. Libraries in Drupal 10 Templates

In Drupal 10, you can use libraries to add CSS and JavaScript files to your custom templates. Libraries allow you to easily include third-party libraries, such as jQuery or Bootstrap, in your templates without having to write custom code to do so.

To use a library in a Drupal 10 template, you first need to define the library in a .libraries.yml file in your theme. Here's an example of how to define a library for the Bootstrap framework:

```
bootstrap:
  version: 4.6.0
  css:
    theme:
      css/bootstrap.min.css: {}
  js:
    bootstrap.min.js: {}
  dependencies:
    - core/jquery
```

In this example, we're defining a library called bootstrap that depends on the jQuery library. The library includes a CSS file and a JavaScript file for the Bootstrap framework.

Once you've defined your library, you can then include it in your template using the attach_library function. Here's an example of how to include the bootstrap library in a Drupal 10 template:

```
{% extends "page.html.twig" %}

{% block content %}
  <h1>Welcome to my site!</h1>
{% endblock %}

{% block footer %}
```

```
{{ attach_library('mytheme/bootstrap') }}
{% endblock %}
```

In this example, we're extending the page.html.twig template and including the bootstrap library in the footer block of our custom template.

By using libraries in your Drupal 10 templates, you can easily add third-party CSS and JavaScript files to your site without having to write custom code to do so. This allows you to create custom templates that are more visually appealing and provide a better user experience for your site's visitors.

4.5.4. Preprocessors in Drupal 10 Templates

Preprocessors, such as Gulp or Webpack, allow you to automate tasks in your development workflow, such as compiling Sass files or minifying JavaScript files. By using preprocessors with Drupal 10, you can streamline your development workflow and save time on repetitive tasks.

To use a preprocessor with Drupal 10, you first need to install it on your local development environment. Once you have installed your preprocessor, you can then create a gulpfile.js or webpack.config.js file in your Drupal 10 theme directory to configure your preprocessor tasks.

For example, let's say you want to use Gulp to compile Sass files in your Drupal 10 theme. Here's an example gulpfile.js file that would accomplish that:

```
var gulp = require('gulp');
var sass = require('gulp-sass');

gulp.task('sass', function() {
  return gulp.src('scss/**/*.scss')
    .pipe(sass().on('error', sass.logError))
    .pipe(gulp.dest('css'));
});

gulp.task('watch', function() {
  gulp.watch('scss/**/*.scss', ['sass']);
});); });
```

In this example, we're defining two Gulp tasks: sass, which compiles Sass files into CSS files, and watch, which watches for changes to Sass files and automatically runs the sass task when changes are detected.

To run your Gulp tasks, you can use the command line to navigate to your theme directory and run the following command:

```
gulp watch
```

By running this command, Gulp will watch for changes to your Sass files and automatically compile them into CSS files whenever changes are detected.

By using preprocessors like Gulp or Webpack with Drupal 10, you can automate repetitive tasks in your development workflow and streamline your development process. This allows you to focus on creating custom templates that meet the specific needs of your site's visitors, without having to worry about the technical details of compiling Sass files or minifying JavaScript files.

4.5.5. Styling (CSS) in Drupal 10 Templates

CSS is an essential component of any Drupal 10 template, as it allows you to style your HTML content and create visually appealing and engaging templates. In Drupal 10, you can add custom CSS to your templates in several ways.

Inline CSS

One way to add custom CSS to your Drupal 10 templates is by using inline CSS. This involves adding the CSS directly to your HTML markup, using the style attribute. For example, to change the font color of a heading in your template, you can use the following code:

```
<h1 style="color: red;">Hello World</h1>lo World</h1>
```

While inline CSS can be a quick and easy way to add custom styles to your templates, it can also make your markup more difficult to read and maintain.

External CSS

A better way to add custom CSS to your Drupal 10 templates is by using external CSS files. This involves creating a separate CSS file and linking to it from your template. For example, to create a separate CSS file for your Drupal 10 theme, you can create a file called style.css in your theme directory and add the following code:

```
h1 {
  color: red;
}
```

You can then link to this CSS file from your Drupal 10 template by adding the following code to the head section of your template:

```
{% block styles %}
  {{ attach_css(theme|theme_path ~ '/css/style.css') }}
{% endblock %}
```

This will include your style.css file in the head section of your Drupal 10 template.

CSS Preprocessors

Another option for styling your Drupal 10 templates is by using a CSS preprocessor, such as Sass or Less. CSS preprocessors allow you to write CSS in a more efficient and organized way, by providing features such as variables, mixins, and nesting.

To use a CSS preprocessor with Drupal 10, you first need to install it on your local development environment. Once you have installed your CSS preprocessor, you can then create a .scss or .less file in your Drupal 10 theme directory and write your CSS using the preprocessor syntax.

For example, let's say you want to use Sass to create custom styles for your Drupal 10 template. Here's an example Sass code that would accomplish that:

```
$primary-color: #f00;

h1 {
  color: $primary-color;
}
```

In this example, we're defining a variable called $primary-color and using it to set the color of a heading in our template. To compile this Sass code into CSS, you can use a preprocessor tool, such as Gulp or Webpack, as described in the previous subcategory.

By using external CSS files or CSS preprocessors in your Drupal 10 templates, you can create custom styles that are easier to read, maintain, and organize. This allows you to create visually stunning and engaging templates that meet the specific needs of your site's visitors.

4.6. Advanced Topics in Layout and Theming

4.6.1. Template Suggestions

Template suggestions allow you to create custom templates for specific types of content or pages on your Drupal 10 site. By defining template suggestions, you can customize the look and feel of your site without having to modify the core templates.

In Drupal 10, you can define template suggestions by creating a file with a specific naming convention in your theme directory. The naming convention is based on the type of content or page that you want to create a custom template for.

For example, to create a custom template for a specific content type on your Drupal 10 site, you can create a file called node--content-type.html.twig in your theme directory, where content-type is the machine name of your content type. This template will be used to render nodes of the specified content type.

4.6.2. Twig Debugging

Twig is the template engine used by Drupal 10 to render HTML markup. By default, Drupal 10 does not show the names of the templates that are used to render each page or block on your site. However, you can enable Twig debugging to display this information in the HTML output of your site.

To enable Twig debugging, you can add the following code to your settings.php file in your Drupal 10 site's sites/default directory:

```
$config['twig.config']['debug'] = TRUE;
$config['twig.config']['auto_reload'] = TRUE;
```

Once you have enabled Twig debugging, you can view the names of the templates that are used to render each page or block by inspecting the HTML output of your site using your browser's developer tools.

4.6.3. Template Inheritance

Template inheritance allows you to create templates that share common elements, such as a header or footer. By using template inheritance, you can define a base template that includes common elements, and then create child templates that extend the base template and add additional content.

In Drupal 10, you can use template inheritance by creating a base template and then creating child templates that extend the base template. To create a child template that extends a base template, you can use the extends keyword in the child template and specify the name of the base template.

Here's an example of a base template that includes a header and footer:

```
<!DOCTYPE html>
<html>
 <head>
  <title>{% block title %}{% endblock %}</title>
 </head>
 <body>
  {% block header %}
   <header>
    <h1>Welcome to my site!</h1>
   </header>
  {% endblock %}

  {% block content %}{% endblock %}

  {% block footer %}
   <footer>
    <p>&copy; 2023 My Site</p>
   </footer>
  {% endblock %}
 </body>
</html>
```

To create a child template that extends this base template and adds additional content, you can use the following code in the child template:

```
{% extends "base.html.twig" %}

{% block title %}My Custom Template{% endblock %}

{% block content %}
  <h1>Welcome to my custom template!</h1>
  <p>This is my custom template content.</p>
{% endblock %}
```

In this example, we're creating a child template that extends the base.html.twig template and adds additional content to the content block. By using template inheritance in this way, we can create templates that are more modular, reusable, and maintainable.

4.6.4. Asset Management

In Drupal 10, you can manage CSS and JavaScript assets (e.g. stylesheets, scripts) using the libraries system. The libraries system allows you to define collections of assets that can be included on specific pages or throughout your site.

To define a library in Drupal 10, you can create a .libraries.yml file in your theme directory. Here's an example of a .libraries.yml file that defines a library called mytheme:

```
mytheme:
  version: 1.x
  css:
    theme:
      css/styles.css: {}
  js:
    js/scripts.js: {}}
```

In this example, we're defining a library called mytheme that
includes a CSS file called css/styles.css and a JavaScript file
called js/scripts.js. Once you have defined a library, you can
include it on specific pages or throughout your site by using the
attach_library function in your theme's templates or preprocess
functions.

4.6.5. Theming Forms

In Drupal 10, you can customize the look and feel of forms on
your site by using form templates. Form templates allow you to
customize the markup and styling of form elements, such as text
fields, checkboxes, and radio buttons.

To create a custom form template in Drupal 10, you can create a
file called form--form-id.html.twig in your theme directory, where
form-id is the machine name of the form you want to customize.
This template will be used to render the specified form.

Here's an example of a form template that customizes the
markup of a text field:

```
{% extends "form.html.twig" %}

{% block textfield %}
  <div class="form-item">
    <label{{ label_attributes }}>{{ label }}</label>
    <input{{ attributes }} />
  </div>
{% endblock %}
```

In this example, we're customizing the markup of the text field by overriding the textfield block in the form.html.twig template. By using form templates in this way, you can create forms that are more consistent with the design of your site.

4.6.6. Twig Extensions

Twig extensions allow you to extend the functionality of Twig by creating custom filters, functions, or tags. Drupal 10 comes with several built-in Twig extensions, such as the url filter for generating URLs, the trans filter for translating text, and the clean_class filter for sanitizing class names.

To create a custom Twig extension in Drupal 10, you can define a service that implements the Twig_ExtensionInterface interface. Here's an example of a Twig extension that defines a custom filter:

```
namespace Drupal\my_module\Twig;
```

```php
use Twig\Extension\AbstractExtension;
use Twig\TwigFilter;

class MyModuleTwigExtension extends AbstractExtension
{

  public function getFilters() {
    return [
      new TwigFilter('my_custom_filter', [$this,
'myCustomFilter']),
    ];
  }

  public function myCustomFilter($string) {
    return strtoupper($string);
  }
}}
```

In this example, we're creating a custom Twig extension that
defines a filter called my_custom_filter. This filter will convert
the input string to uppercase. Once you have defined a Twig
extension, you can register it as a service in your Drupal 10 site's
services.yml file and use it in your Twig templates.

By using the techniques described above, you can create custom
templates that are more flexible, maintainable, and powerful in
Drupal

4.6.7. Twig Caching

Twig caching allows you to speed up the rendering of your Drupal 10 site's templates by caching the compiled Twig templates in the Drupal cache. By caching the compiled templates, Drupal 10 can avoid the overhead of compiling the templates on every page request, which can significantly improve the performance of your site.

To enable Twig caching in Drupal 10, you can add the following code to your settings.php file in your Drupal 10 site's sites/default directory:

```
$settings['cache']['bins']['twig'] = 'cache.backend.null';
```

Once you have enabled Twig caching, Drupal 10 will cache the compiled Twig templates in the Drupal cache. You can clear the Twig cache by clearing the Drupal cache using the drush cache:rebuild or drupal cache:rebuild command.

4.6.8. Twig Security

Twig security allows you to restrict access to certain Twig functions, filters, and tags to improve the security of your Drupal 10 site. By restricting access to certain Twig functions, filters, and tags, you can prevent users from executing malicious code or accessing sensitive data.

To configure Twig security in Drupal 10, you can add the following code to your services.yml file in your Drupal 10 site's sites/default directory:

```
twig.config:
  security_policy:
    disallowed_tags: []
    allowed_tags: ['if', 'for', 'set']
    disallowed_functions: ['exec', 'passthru', 'shell_exec',
'system', 'eval']
    allowed_functions: []]
```

In this example, we're configuring Twig security to disallow the execution of certain functions (exec, passthru, shell_exec, system, and eval) and only allow the use of certain tags (if, for, and set). By using Twig security in this way, you can improve the security of your Drupal 10 site and prevent users from executing malicious code.

4.6.9. Theming Regions

In Drupal 10, you can define regions in your theme that can be used to place blocks or other content on your site's pages. To define a region in Drupal 10, you can add the following code to your theme's .info.yml file:

```
regions:
  header: 'Header'
```

```
content: 'Content'
sidebar: 'Sidebar'
footer: 'Footer'
```

In this example, we're defining four regions (header, content, sidebar, and footer) in our theme. Once you have defined regions in your theme, you can use the region function in your theme's templates to output the content of a specific region. For example, you can use the following code in your page.html.twig template to output the content of the header region:

```
{% if page.header %}
  <header>
    {{ page.header }}
  </header>
{% endif %}
```

By using regions in your theme, you can create more flexible and modular layouts for your Drupal 10 site.

4.6.10. Template Suggestions

Template suggestions allow you to customize the markup and styling of specific pages, nodes, or other entities on your site. By using template suggestions, you can create templates that are more specific to the content you are rendering, which can help you create more unique and visually appealing designs.

To create a custom template suggestion in Drupal 10, you can use the following naming conventions for your template files:

- For pages: page--path--to--page.html.twig
- For nodes: node--node-type.html.twig
- For blocks: block--block-id.html.twig
- For views: views-view--view-id--display-id.html.twig

In each of these examples, you can replace path--to--page, node-type, block-id, view-id, and display-id with the appropriate values for your page, node, block, or view.

For example, if you wanted to create a custom template for a specific content type (e.g. "Article"), you could create a file called node--article.html.twig in your theme's templates directory. This template would be used to render any nodes of the "Article" content type.

4.6.11. Twig Debugging

Twig debugging allows you to debug issues with your Drupal 10 site's templates by providing additional information about the templates that are being used to render the page. By enabling Twig debugging, you can see a list of all the templates that were used to render the current page, as well as the variables that are available in each template.

To enable Twig debugging in Drupal 10, you can add the following code to your settings.php file in your Drupal 10 site's sites/default directory:

```
$settings['twig_debug'] = TRUE;
```

Once you have enabled Twig debugging, you can view the Twig debugging information by adding ?_twig_debug to the end of the URL for any page on your site. This will display a list of all the templates that were used to render the page, as well as the variables that are available in each template.

4.6.12. Theming Contributed Modules

Contributed modules in Drupal 10 may provide their own templates and theme functions that you can use to customize the output of the module. To override a contributed module's template or theme function in your theme, you can follow the same naming conventions as for core templates and theme functions.

For example, if a contributed module called "MyModule" provides a template called my-module.html.twig, you can override this template in your theme by creating a file called my-module.html.twig in your theme's templates directory. Once you have created this file, your theme's version of the template will be used instead of the contributed module's version.

By using these techniques, you can create more customized and visually appealing designs for your Drupal 10 site.

4.6.13. Twig Filters

Twig filters allow you to modify the output of variables in your Drupal 10 site's templates. By using Twig filters, you can transform or format variables in a variety of ways to meet your needs.

Some commonly used Twig filters in Drupal 10 include:

- raw: Renders a variable without escaping any HTML or special characters.
- date: Formats a date variable according to a specific format.
- number_format: Formats a number variable with a specified number of decimal places and thousands separator.
- length: Returns the length of a variable (e.g. the number of characters in a string).

To use a Twig filter in your Drupal 10 site's templates, you can add the filter name to the end of the variable you want to modify, followed by a pipe symbol (|). For example, you could use the following code to format a date variable:

```
{{ node.createdtime|date('F j, Y') }}
```

This code would format the createdtime variable as a human-readable date string (e.g. "January 1, 2022").

4.6.14. Twig Functions

Twig functions allow you to execute custom PHP code in your Drupal 10 site's templates. By using Twig functions, you can add more complex logic or functionality to your templates that cannot be achieved with Twig filters alone.

Some commonly used Twig functions in Drupal 10 include:

- url: Generates a URL for a given route or path.
- drupal_set_title: Sets the title of the current page.
- drupal_get_messages: Retrieves any messages (e.g. status, warning, or error messages) that have been set by other modules or parts of Drupal.

To use a Twig function in your Drupal 10 site's templates, you can call the function name followed by parentheses and any required arguments. For example, you could use the following code to generate a URL for a given route:

This code would generate a link to the canonical URL for node 123 on your Drupal 10 site.

4.6.15. Debugging Twig Templates

If you encounter issues with your Drupal 10 site's templates, you can use the built-in Twig debugging tools to help identify and resolve the issues. To enable Twig debugging, you can add the following code to your Drupal 10 site's settings.php file:

Once you have enabled Twig debugging, you can view additional debugging information by appending ?_twig_debug to the end of the URL for any page on your site. This will display a list of all the templates that were used to render the page, as well as any variables that were passed to each template.

By using these techniques, you can create more dynamic, customized, and visually appealing designs for your Drupal 10 site.

4.6.16. Twig Variables

Twig variables allow you to access and manipulate data in your Drupal 10 site's templates. There are a wide variety of Twig variables available in Drupal 10, including variables for nodes, users, menus, and more.

To view a list of available Twig variables on a given page of your Drupal 10 site, you can use the dump function. For example, you could use the following code to view all available Twig variables on a page:

This code would output a formatted list of all available Twig variables on the current page.

4.6.17. Twig Extensions

Twig extensions are custom classes that allow you to add new functionality to your Drupal 10 site's templates. By creating your own Twig extensions, you can extend the capabilities of Twig and create more complex and powerful templates.

To create a custom Twig extension in Drupal 10, you can create a new PHP class that extends the Twig_Extension class, and implement any necessary methods. Once you have created your extension class, you can register it with Drupal 10 using the twig.extension service.

4.6.18. Twig Best Practices

There are a number of best practices that you can follow when working with Twig templates in Drupal 10, including:

- Keep your templates modular and reusable.
- Use template inheritance to avoid duplicating code.
- Use template suggestions to create more specific templates.
- Use Twig filters and functions to transform and manipulate data.
- Use Twig debugging to identify and resolve issues with your templates.
- Use caching to improve the performance of your templates.

By following these best practices, you can create more efficient, maintainable, and effective templates for your Drupal 10 site.

4.6.19. Twig Namespaces

Twig namespaces allow you to organize your templates into different namespaces or groups. This can be helpful when you have a large number of templates or when you want to separate templates by functionality.

To define a new Twig namespace in your Drupal 10 site, you can add the following code to your theme_name.theme file:

```
$loader = new \Twig\Loader\FilesystemLoader([
  $theme_path . '/templates',
  $module_path . '/templates',
]);
$twig->getLoader()->addLoader($loader);
```

In this example, we are defining a new namespace called my_custom_namespace and adding two directories to it: themes/custom/my_theme/templates and modules/my_module/templates. Once you have defined your Twig namespace, you can use it in your templates like this:

```
{% extends '@my_custom_namespace/base.html.twig' %}
```

This code would extend the base.html.twig template in the my_custom_namespace namespace.

4.6.20. Twig Profiler

The Twig profiler is a built-in tool in Drupal 10 that allows you to analyze the performance of your Twig templates. The profiler provides information on template rendering time, memory usage, and cache hits/misses, as well as other metrics.

> The Twig profiler is a built-in tool in Drupal 10 that allows you to analyze the performance of your Twig templates. The profiler provides information on template rendering time, memory usage, and cache hits/misses, as well as other metrics.

Once you have enabled the Twig profiler, you can view profiling information by appending ?_twig_profile to the end of the URL for any page on your site. This will display a detailed report of the Twig templates that were used to render the page, as well as performance metrics for each template.

4.6.21. Theming Hooks

Theming hooks are functions that allow you to modify the output of various parts of your Drupal 10 site's templates. By using theming hooks, you can add or modify HTML, CSS, or JavaScript code in your templates to achieve a specific look or functionality.

There are a large number of theming hooks available in Drupal 10, including hooks for nodes, blocks, forms, and more. To use a theming hook in your Drupal 10 site, you can create a new function in your theme_name.theme file with a specific name, and Drupal will automatically call that function when the corresponding template is rendered.

4.6.28. Using Base Themes

Base themes are pre-existing themes in Drupal 10 that can be used as a starting point for building your own custom theme. By using a base theme, you can save time and effort by leveraging existing code and styling.

To use a base theme in Drupal 10, you can create a new theme that extends the base theme. You can do this by adding the following code to your theme_name.info.yml file:

```
name: My Custom Theme
type: theme
description: 'Custom Drupal 10 theme based on the Bartik theme'
core_version_requirement: ^8 || ^9 || ^10
base theme: bartik
```

In this example, we are creating a new theme called "My Custom Theme" that is based on the built-in "Bartik" theme. Once you have created your theme, you can modify the templates, CSS, and other files as needed to customize the look and feel of your site.

4.6.29. Theme Hook Suggestions

Theme hook suggestions are a way to provide additional template files for specific elements on your site. For example, you might want to create a custom template file for a specific block or form element.

To create a theme hook suggestion in Drupal 10, you can use the following naming convention:

```
[base hook name]--[suggestion].html.twig
```

For example, if you want to create a new template suggestion for the "login" block, you could create a template file called block--user-login.html.twig. Drupal 10 will automatically use this template for the "login" block.

You can also create theme hook suggestions for other elements, such as form elements or views. For more information on creating theme hook suggestions, see the Drupal 10 documentation.

4.6.30. Using Conditional Stylesheets

Conditional stylesheets are a technique in Drupal 10 that allow you to specify different CSS files for different conditions, such as the user's browser or device. This can be helpful when you need to optimize your site for different types of users or devices.

To use a conditional stylesheet in Drupal 10, you can add the following code to your theme_name.info.yml file:

```
stylesheets-conditional:
  lt-ie9:
    css/layout-ie.css: { browser: 'IE', version: 'lt IE 9' }
```

In this example, we are creating a new conditional stylesheet for users with Internet Explorer 8 or below. The lt-ie9 value is the name of the condition, and the css/layout-ie.css value is the path to the CSS file. The browser and version values specify the conditions under which the stylesheet should be loaded.

You can also use conditional stylesheets to load different stylesheets based on other conditions, such as the user's device type or screen size. For more information on using conditional stylesheets, see the Drupal 10 documentation.

Chapter 5: Extending Drupal Functionality

Drupal 10 provides a powerful platform for building custom functionality and extending the core features of the platform. In this chapter, we will explore some of the most common ways to extend Drupal, including:

- Using Composer to Install and Manage Modules
- Creating Custom Modules

Using Composer to Install and Manage Modules:

In Drupal 10, it is recommended to use Composer to download and manage modules instead of downloading them manually. Composer is a dependency management tool for PHP that helps you keep track of which modules you are using and ensures that their dependencies are installed correctly.

To use Composer to download modules in Drupal 10, you will first need to install Composer on your system. Once you have installed Composer, you can create a new Drupal 10 project and use the composer require command to download and install modules. Composer will automatically download the module and its dependencies and place them in the correct directories in your Drupal 10 project.

Creating Custom Modules:

In addition to using contributed modules, you can also create your own custom modules in Drupal 10. Custom modules can be used to add specific features or functionality to your site that is not available in existing modules.

To create a custom module in Drupal 10, you will need to have some programming experience in PHP. Drupal 10 uses the Symfony framework, so you will also need to be familiar with Symfony concepts such as services, routing, and controllers.

Once you have created a custom module, you can enable and configure it on the "Extend" page, and use it to add new functionality to your site. With the ability to create and install custom modules using Composer, Drupal 10 provides a flexible and powerful way to extend and customize your site to meet your specific needs.

5.1. An Introduction to Modules

Modules are packages of code that can be installed on a Drupal site to add new functionality or modify existing features. In Drupal 10, there are thousands of contributed modules available, ranging from simple utility modules to full-featured site builders.

Modules can be used to add features like search engine optimization, contact forms, image galleries, and social media integration. They can also be used to modify core functionality, such as altering the way content is displayed or creating custom user roles and permissions.

Drupal 10 includes a number of core modules that provide basic functionality, such as the ability to create and manage content, user accounts, and taxonomy terms. Contributed modules are available from the Drupal website or via Composer, and can be installed and enabled through the Drupal admin interface.

Modules can be configured and customized through the admin interface or by modifying their code directly. Many modules also provide hooks that allow other modules or custom code to interact with their functionality.

In the next section, we will explore how to install and manage modules in Drupal 10 using Composer.

5.2. Installing and Configuring Modules

In Drupal 10, there are two main ways to install and configure modules: using the built-in module installer in the Drupal admin interface, or using Composer to manage module dependencies.

Using the Module Installer:

To install a module using the built-in module installer, navigate to the "Extend" page in the Drupal admin interface. From there, you can search for modules by name, filter by category, or browse the full list of available modules. Once you have found the module you want to install, simply click the "Install" button next to its name.

Some modules may have configuration options that can be set after installation. These options can be accessed by clicking the "Configure" button next to the module on the "Extend" page.

Using Composer:

Using Composer to manage module dependencies is the recommended approach in Drupal 10, as it ensures that the correct versions of each module are installed and that any necessary dependencies are included. To install a module using Composer, simply navigate to your Drupal site's root directory and run the command "composer require [module_name]". This will download and install the module and any required dependencies.

Once you have installed a module, you can enable and configure it on the "Extend" page in the Drupal admin interface. Some modules may also provide additional configuration options or settings pages that can be accessed through the Drupal admin interface.

When installing and configuring modules, it is important to keep in mind that some modules may conflict with each other or with core Drupal functionality. It is always a good idea to test new modules on a development or staging site before deploying them to a live production site.

5.2.1. Enabling and Disabling Modules

Once you have installed a module, you can enable it on the "Extend" page in the Drupal admin interface. To enable a module, simply check the box next to its name and click the "Install" button at the bottom of the page.

After a module has been enabled, you can configure its settings by clicking the "Configure" button next to its name on the "Extend" page. The configuration options for each module will vary depending on the module's functionality.

If you no longer need a module, you can disable it on the "Extend" page by unchecking the box next to its name and clicking the "Uninstall" button. Disabling a module will remove its functionality from your site, but will not delete any data associated with the module (such as content types or fields).

It is important to note that disabling or uninstalling a module may have unintended consequences if the module is being used by other modules or custom code. It is always a good idea to test the effects of disabling or uninstalling a module on a development or staging site before making changes to a live production site.

5.2.1. Updating Drupal Core and Modules

In Drupal 10, you can use Composer to update both Drupal core and modules.

To update Drupal core, navigate to your Drupal site's root directory and run the command "composer update drupal/core-recommended". This will download and install the latest version of Drupal core and any required dependencies.

To update modules, navigate to your Drupal site's root directory and run the command "composer update drupal/[module_name]". This will download and install the latest version of the specified module and any required dependencies.

Before updating Drupal core or modules, it is important to review the release notes and documentation for each update to ensure that there are no known issues or conflicts with your site's configuration or other modules. It is also recommended to test updates on a development or staging site before deploying them to a live production site.

Finally, it is important to regularly check for updates to Drupal core and modules in order to ensure the security and stability of your site.

5.2.3. Uninstalling Modules

If you no longer need a module on your Drupal site, you can uninstall it using the "Uninstall" tab on the "Extend" page in the Drupal admin interface.

To uninstall a module, simply click the "Uninstall" tab on the "Extend" page and check the box next to the module you want to uninstall. Then click the "Uninstall" button at the bottom of the page. Drupal will remove all data associated with the module, including any content types, fields, and configuration settings.

It is important to note that uninstalling a module may have unintended consequences if the module is being used by other modules or custom code. It is always a good idea to test the effects of uninstalling a module on a development or staging site before making changes to a live production site.

If you later decide that you need to use a module that you previously uninstalled, you can reinstall it by following the instructions for installing and enabling modules. However, any data that was previously associated with the module (such as content types or fields) will need to be recreated.

It is important to keep your Drupal site clean and free of unused modules in order to ensure the security and stability of your site. Uninstalling modules that are no longer needed can also help to improve the performance of your site.

5.3. Essential Modules for Drupal 10

While Drupal 10 provides a lot of functionality out of the box, there are several essential modules that can help to extend and enhance your site. Here are a few popular modules that are recommended for almost any Drupal 10 site:

- Pathauto: This module automatically generates clean, SEO-friendly URLs for your content based on the title of the page or post. This can help to improve your site's search engine optimization and make your URLs more readable and memorable for visitors.
- Metatag: This module provides an easy way to manage meta tags and other important HTML tags for your site, including the meta description, keywords, and social media sharing tags. This can help to improve your site's search engine optimization and social media sharing capabilities.
- Views: This module provides a powerful and flexible way to display lists of content on your site, including posts, pages, and custom content types. It allows you to customize the layout and formatting of your content, as well as filter and sort content based on various criteria.
- Token: This module provides a system for creating and managing dynamic tokens in Drupal. These tokens can be used in various places throughout your site, such as in paths, content, and email messages, and can be

automatically replaced with the appropriate content when viewed by a user.

- Webform: This module provides an easy way to create and manage forms on your Drupal site, including contact forms, surveys, and more. It includes a drag-and-drop form builder, as well as support for conditional logic and advanced field types.

These are just a few examples of the essential modules that can help to extend and enhance your Drupal 10 site. There are many other modules available for Drupal 10, including contributed modules that provide additional functionality and customization options. When selecting modules for your site, it's important to review their features and compatibility with your site's version of Drupal, as well as their user ratings and reviews.

5.3.1 Installing Essential Modules

To install essential modules for Drupal 10, the recommended method is to use Composer. Composer is a dependency manager for PHP that allows you to easily manage dependencies and packages for your Drupal site. It is the recommended way to install and manage Drupal core and contributed modules.

To get started, you will need to have Composer installed on your system. You can download and install Composer from the official website at https://getcomposer.org.

Once you have Composer installed, you can use the require command to download and install the modules you need. For example, to install the Pathauto module, you can run the following command in your Drupal site's root directory:

`composer require drupal/pathauto`

This command will download and install the latest version of the Pathauto module, as well as any dependencies it requires. You can replace drupal/pathauto with the name of any other module you want to install.

After the module is installed, you will need to enable it in your Drupal site's admin panel. To do this, navigate to the "Extend" page and find the module you just installed in the list. Check the box next to the module and click the "Install" button to enable it.

Once the module is enabled, you can configure its settings by navigating to the module's configuration page. Each module will have its own configuration options, which you can access from the "Configuration" page in your site's admin panel.

Remember to review the documentation for each module you install to ensure that you are using it correctly and taking advantage of all its features.

5.3.2 Updating Essential Modules

It is important to keep your Drupal 10 site and all its modules up to date in order to ensure the security and stability of your site. When new updates are released for essential modules, it is recommended that you update them as soon as possible.

To update essential modules, you can use Composer's update command. This command will download and install the latest version of each module, as well as any dependencies or required updates.

To update all installed modules, run the following command in your Drupal site's root directory:

This command will update all installed modules and their dependencies to the latest compatible version. If there are any updates available for a module, Composer will automatically download and install them.

After updating your modules, it's important to test your site to ensure that everything is working correctly. Check your site's functionality and test any custom code or integrations to ensure that they are still working as expected.

Remember to review the release notes and documentation for each updated module to ensure that you are using it correctly and taking advantage of any new features or improvements.

5.3.3 Essential Modules for Site Building

Essential modules are those that are commonly used in building Drupal sites. These modules provide additional functionality and features that can enhance the capabilities of your site.

Some of the essential modules for site building in Drupal 10 include:

- **Views**: a powerful module that allows you to create custom lists, grids, tables, and more to display your site's content
- **Token**: a module that provides a system for generating placeholder values for dynamic data
- **Pathauto**: a module that automatically generates human-readable URLs for your site's content
- **Metatag**: a module that allows you to add meta tags to your site's pages, which can help with search engine optimization (SEO)

- **Webform**: a module that provides a drag-and-drop interface for creating forms on your site
- **Redirect**: a module that allows you to create and manage URL redirects on your site

These modules are just a few examples of the many essential modules available for Drupal 10. Depending on your site's needs and requirements, you may need to use additional modules to provide the functionality and features you need.

When selecting and installing modules for your site, be sure to review the documentation and requirements for each module to ensure that it is compatible with your version of Drupal and any other modules you have installed. Additionally, keep in mind the impact that additional modules can have on your site's performance and security, and only install those that are truly necessary.

5.3.4 Contributing to the Drupal Community

Drupal is an open-source platform, which means that its development is driven by a community of contributors. If you are interested in contributing to the Drupal community, there are several ways to get involved.

One way to contribute to Drupal is to participate in the community forums or attend local Drupal events. This is a great way to connect with other Drupal users and developers, learn about new developments in the platform, and get help with any issues you may be experiencing.

Another way to contribute to the Drupal community is to create and share your own modules and themes. By making your code available to others, you can help to extend the functionality of Drupal and make it a more versatile and powerful platform.

If you are interested in contributing to the core development of Drupal, you can get involved with the Drupal Association, which oversees the development of the platform. The Drupal Association welcomes contributions from developers of all skill levels, and provides a range of resources and tools to help you get started.

By contributing to the Drupal community, you can help to ensure the ongoing development and success of the platform, and make it an even better tool for building powerful and scalable websites.

5.3.5 Maintaining Your Modules

Once you have installed and configured your modules, it is important to keep them up-to-date to ensure the security and stability of your site. This involves monitoring for new module releases, testing updates in a development environment, and applying updates to your live site.

To keep your modules up-to-date, you can use Drupal's Update Manager, which provides notifications of available updates for your installed modules. You can also manually check for updates by visiting the project pages of your installed modules on Drupal.org.

When updating your modules, it is important to test the updates in a development environment before applying them to your live site. This can help to identify any compatibility issues or conflicts with other modules or custom code on your site. Once you have tested the updates and ensured that they are compatible with your site, you can apply them to your live site.

In addition to keeping your modules up-to-date, it is important to periodically review your installed modules and remove any that are no longer needed or are causing compatibility issues or security vulnerabilities. By keeping your modules well-maintained, you can help to ensure the long-term stability and security of your Drupal site.

5.4. Creating Custom Modules

While Drupal provides a wide range of modules to extend the functionality of your site, there may be cases where you need to create your own custom module to meet your specific requirements.

Creating a custom module involves several steps, including creating a module directory, defining the module structure and settings, creating custom code and functionality, and testing and deploying the module.

To create a custom module, you can follow these steps:

1. Create a new directory for your module in the sites/all/modules directory of your Drupal installation.

2. Create a new file within your module directory called MODULENAME.info.yml. This file will define the basic information and settings for your module, including the module name, description, version, dependencies, and any other required settings.

3. Create a new file within your module directory called MODULENAME.module. This file will contain the main code and functionality for your module.

4. Define the functionality and behavior of your module using Drupal's API functions and hooks. This can involve defining new content types, creating custom fields, implementing new user roles and permissions, and more.

5. Test your module to ensure that it is functioning as intended and is compatible with your site's existing modules and functionality.

6. Deploy your module to your site's production environment, either by manually copying the module files or by using a version control system like Git.

By creating custom modules, you can extend the functionality of your Drupal site and meet your specific requirements, while also gaining valuable experience in Drupal development and contributing to the Drupal community.

5.4.1. Creating a Basic Module

To get started with creating a custom module in Drupal 10, you can create a basic module that includes a simple "Hello, World!" message.

Here are the steps to create a basic module:

1. Create a new directory for your module in the sites/all/modules directory of your Drupal installation. You can name the directory anything you like, but for this example, we'll use helloworld.

2. Within the helloworld directory, create a new file called helloworld.info.yml. This file should include the following code:

   This code defines the basic information and settings for your module, including the module name, description, package, type, and required Drupal core version.

3. Within the helloworld directory, create a new file called helloworld.module. This file should include the following code:

```php
<?php

/**
 * Implements hook_help().
 */
function helloworld_help($route_name, $route_parameters) {
  switch ($route_name) {
    case 'help.page.helloworld':
      $output = '';
      $output .= '<h3>' . t('About') . '</h3>';
      $output .= '<p>' . t('This module outputs a greeting
message.') . '</p>';
      return $output;

    default:
  }
}

/**
 * Implements hook_menu().
 */
function helloworld_menu() {
  $items['hello'] = array(
    'title' => 'Hello, World!',
    'page callback' => 'helloworld_hello',
    'access arguments' => array('access content'),
  );

  return $items;
}

/**
 * Page callback function for /hello.
```

```
*/
function helloworld_hello() {
  return '<h1>Hello, World!</h1>';
}/
```

4. This code defines the main functionality of your module, including the helloworld_help(), helloworld_menu(), and helloworld_hello() functions. The helloworld_help() function defines the help text for your module, the helloworld_menu() function defines a new menu item for your module, and the helloworld_hello() function defines the output of the /hello page.

5. Enable your module by navigating to the "Extend" page of your Drupal site, selecting the "Hello World" module from the list of available modules, and clicking the "Install" button.

6. Visit the /hello page of your Drupal site to see the "Hello, World!" message output by your module.

By creating a basic module, you can gain a better understanding of how to create custom modules in Drupal and extend the functionality of your site in new and unique ways.

5.4.2. Building More Complex Modules

Once you have a good understanding of how to create a basic module in Drupal 10, you can start building more complex modules that include additional functionality and features.

Here are some tips and best practices for building more complex modules:

1. Use the Drupal Console or Drush to generate module scaffolding. Both tools provide a quick and easy way to generate the basic files and structure for a new module, including the .info.yml, .module, and .routing.yml files.

2. Use hooks to extend Drupal's core functionality. Drupal includes a wide range of hooks that allow modules to interact with core functionality and modify the behavior of the site. Some common hooks include hook_block_info(), hook_block_view(), and hook_form_alter().

3. Use the Drupal API to access and manipulate data. Drupal provides a powerful API that allows modules to interact with the site's database and other data sources. The API includes functions for working with nodes, users, taxonomy terms, and more.

4. Use object-oriented programming (OOP) principles to organize and structure your code. Drupal 8 and later versions have embraced OOP principles, and you can take advantage of these principles when building custom modules. Using classes, interfaces, and other OOP concepts can help make your code more modular and easier to maintain.

5. Write clear and concise code that follows Drupal coding standards. Drupal has specific coding standards that all contributed modules should follow, including indentation, spacing, and variable naming conventions. Following these standards can help ensure that your module is easy to read and maintain.

By following these tips and best practices, you can build more complex and powerful modules in Drupal 10 that extend the functionality of your site in new and innovative ways.

5.4.3. Debugging and Troubleshooting Modules

When building custom modules in Drupal 10, it's important to have a good understanding of how to debug and troubleshoot issues that may arise. Here are some tips for debugging and troubleshooting modules:

1. Use Drupal's built-in debugging tools. Drupal 10 includes several built-in debugging tools that can help you identify and troubleshoot issues with your module. For example, you can use the dpm() function to print out the contents of a variable to the screen, or you can use the watchdog() function to log messages to Drupal's database log.

2. Use an integrated development environment (IDE). Using an IDE like PHPStorm or Visual Studio Code can provide helpful debugging features like breakpoints, code profiling, and error highlighting.

3. Check the Drupal logs. Drupal logs all system messages and errors to the database log, which can be accessed from the Drupal admin interface. Checking the logs can help you identify errors and troubleshoot issues with your module.

4. Use Xdebug or other debugging tools. Xdebug is a popular PHP debugging tool that can be used with Drupal to provide advanced debugging features like stack tracing, code profiling, and variable inspection.

5. Test your module on a clean Drupal installation. Testing your module on a clean Drupal installation can help identify issues that may be caused by conflicts with other modules or configuration settings.

By following these tips and best practices, you can more easily debug and troubleshoot issues with your custom modules in Drupal 10, and ensure that they are working as intended.

5.4.4. Security Best Practices for Custom Modules

When creating custom modules in Drupal 10, it's important to follow security best practices to protect your website and its users from potential security vulnerabilities. Here are some tips for ensuring that your custom modules are secure:

1. Validate user input. When accepting user input in your custom module, make sure to validate it thoroughly to prevent malicious input from causing security vulnerabilities.
2. Use Drupal's built-in security features. Drupal 10 includes several built-in security features like password hashing, user roles and permissions, and input sanitization. Make sure to use these features in your custom module to ensure that it is secure.
3. Use secure coding practices. Use secure coding practices like input validation, output sanitization, and SQL injection prevention to protect your custom module from security vulnerabilities.

4. Stay up to date with security updates. Make sure to stay up to date with security updates for Drupal 10 and any third-party libraries or modules used in your custom module to ensure that any security vulnerabilities are patched.

By following these security best practices, you can help ensure that your custom modules are secure and protect your website and its users from potential security vulnerabilities.

5.4.5. Contributing Your Module to Drupal.org

If you've created a custom module for Drupal 10 that you think could be useful to others, you may want to consider contributing it to Drupal.org. Contributing your module to Drupal.org can provide several benefits, including:

1. Increased visibility and exposure for your module.
2. Community support and feedback for your module.
3. Access to Drupal.org's automated testing and packaging tools.

Here are the steps to contribute your module to Drupal.org:

1. Create an account on Drupal.org if you don't already have one.
2. Navigate to the "Add project" page on Drupal.org.
3. Fill out the project information form, including the project name, description, and recommended Drupal core version.
4. Upload your module's code as a zip file or provide a link to your module's code repository.

5. Follow Drupal.org's contribution guidelines and submit your project for review.

Once your project is reviewed and approved by the Drupal.org community, it will be listed in the Drupal.org project directory and can be downloaded and used by other Drupal users.

By contributing your module to Drupal.org, you can help the Drupal community by sharing your knowledge and expertise, and potentially make a valuable contribution to the Drupal ecosystem.

5.4.6. Debugging and Troubleshooting Custom Modules

When creating custom modules in Drupal 10, it's common to encounter issues and errors that need to be debugged and fixed. Here are some tips for debugging and troubleshooting your custom module:

1. Use Drupal's built-in debugging tools. Drupal 10 includes several built-in debugging tools like the Devel module and the Drupal Debugging Console that can help you identify and fix issues in your custom module.
2. Use Xdebug for PHP debugging. Xdebug is a powerful PHP debugging tool that can help you debug complex issues in your custom module's PHP code.
3. Use browser-based debugging tools. Many modern browsers include built-in debugging tools like the Chrome DevTools or Firefox Developer Tools that can help you identify and fix issues in your custom module's JavaScript code.

4. Use error logs. Drupal 10 includes error logging tools that can help you identify and fix issues in your custom module's code.
5. Use a version control system. Using a version control system like Git can help you track changes to your custom module's code and easily revert to previous versions if needed.

By following these tips for debugging and troubleshooting your custom module, you can identify and fix issues quickly and efficiently, and ensure that your module is functioning correctly.

5.4.7. Best Practices for Creating Custom Modules

When creating custom modules in Drupal 10, it's important to follow best practices to ensure that your module is efficient, secure, and easy to maintain. Here are some best practices for creating custom modules in Drupal 10:

1. Use the Drupal coding standards. Drupal has a set of coding standards that all modules should follow to ensure consistency and readability of the code.
2. Use secure coding practices. When creating custom modules, it's important to use secure coding practices to prevent vulnerabilities and attacks.
3. Use Drupal's APIs and hooks. Drupal provides many APIs and hooks that can be used to create functionality within your module. Using these APIs and hooks can save time and ensure compatibility with future Drupal versions.
4. Use version control. Using a version control system like Git can help you track changes to your code and collaborate with other developers.

5. Write clear and comprehensive documentation. Documenting your code can help other developers understand how your module works and how it can be used.

By following these best practices, you can create high-quality custom modules that are efficient, secure, and easy to maintain, and contribute to the overall health and functionality of the Drupal ecosystem.

5.4.8. Contributing to Drupal Modules

Contributing to Drupal modules is a great way to give back to the community and improve the functionality and usability of Drupal. Here are some ways to contribute to Drupal modules:

1. Report issues. If you encounter issues with a Drupal module, report them to the module maintainer. This helps improve the quality of the module and ensures that issues are addressed in a timely manner.
2. Contribute patches. If you've identified a bug or have a fix for an issue, consider contributing a patch to the module's repository. Patches help improve the stability and functionality of the module.
3. Help with documentation. Contributing to a module's documentation can help other developers understand how to use and extend the module.
4. Translate modules. Contributing translations for Drupal modules can help make them accessible to a wider audience.
5. Contribute new features. If you have an idea for a new feature or functionality that would benefit the Drupal community, consider contributing it to an existing module or creating a new module.

By contributing to Drupal modules, you can help improve the functionality and usability of Drupal, and help ensure that the platform remains a valuable resource for developers and users alike.

5.4.9. Drupal Coding Standards

Following Drupal coding standards is important for creating maintainable, readable, and compatible code. Drupal has its own set of coding standards, which include guidelines for formatting, naming conventions, and more. Here are some key aspects of Drupal's coding standards:

1. Formatting. Drupal's coding standards define rules for indentation, line length, whitespace, and more. Consistent formatting helps make code more readable and easier to maintain.
2. Naming conventions. Drupal's coding standards define naming conventions for variables, functions, classes, and more. Consistent naming conventions help make code more understandable and easier to work with.
3. Documentation. Drupal's coding standards require documentation for functions, classes, and other code elements. Documentation helps developers understand the purpose and functionality of code.
4. Security. Drupal's coding standards include guidelines for writing secure code, such as using secure input validation and escaping output.
5. Compatibility. Drupal's coding standards ensure that code is compatible with the Drupal core and other contributed modules.

By following Drupal's coding standards, you can create maintainable, readable, and compatible code that is easier to work with and less prone to errors. Drupal's coding standards are a valuable resource for developers who want to create high-quality Drupal modules and contribute to the Drupal community.

5.4.10. Automated Code Quality Tools: PHPCS and PHPCBF

PHPCS (PHP CodeSniffer) and PHPCBF (PHP Code Beautifier and Fixer) are automated tools that can help ensure your code adheres to Drupal's coding standards. PHPCS is a command-line tool that checks your code against a set of predefined coding standards. PHPCBF is a related tool that automatically fixes common coding standard violations.

To use PHPCS and PHPCBF, you first need to install them on your system. You can install both tools using Composer, like this:

```
composer require squizlabs/php_codesniffer
```

Once you have installed PHPCS, you can use it to check your code for coding standard violations. For example, you can run the following command to check a module file:

```
vendor/bin/phpcs path/to/your/module/module_name
```

PHPCS will output a report of any coding standard violations it finds.

If you want to automatically fix coding standard violations, you can use PHPCBF. For example, you can run the following command to fix coding standard violations in a module file:

```
vendor/bin/phpcbf path/to/your/module/module_name
```

PHPCBF will automatically fix common coding standard violations, such as whitespace issues and indentation errors.

Using PHPCS and PHPCBF can help ensure that your code adheres to Drupal's coding standards, making your code easier to maintain and less prone to errors. By incorporating these tools into your development workflow, you can save time and improve the quality of your code.

5.4.11. Debugging Drupal Code

Debugging code is an important part of development, and Drupal provides several tools to help you debug your code. Here are some of the most common tools and techniques for debugging Drupal code:

1. Devel module: The Devel module is a popular tool for debugging Drupal code. It provides several useful functions for debugging, such as dpm(), which prints out the value of a variable in a nicely formatted way.

2. Xdebug: Xdebug is a powerful debugging tool for PHP that can be used with Drupal. It allows you to step through your code, set breakpoints, and view the state of your variables at different points in your code.

3. Drupal's logging system: Drupal provides a logging system that can be used to log errors, warnings, and other messages. By default, Drupal logs messages to the database, but you can also configure it to log to a file or an external service.

4. Browser-based debugging: Modern browsers provide powerful debugging tools that can be used to debug JavaScript and CSS. By using the browser's developer tools, you can inspect HTML and CSS, debug JavaScript code, and view network traffic.

5. Debugging database queries: Drupal provides a database abstraction layer that makes it easy to work with databases. If you're experiencing performance issues or other problems related to database queries, you can use Drupal's query logging system to log and analyze database queries.

By using these tools and techniques, you can more easily debug your Drupal code and identify and fix issues quickly.

5.4.12. Testing Drupal Code

Testing your code is an essential part of development, and Drupal provides several tools and techniques for testing your code. Here are some of the most common tools and techniques for testing Drupal code:

1. **Simpletest**: Simpletest is a testing framework built into Drupal that allows you to write automated tests for your code. Simpletest provides several useful functions for testing Drupal code, such as drupalGet() and drupalPost(), which simulate HTTP requests to your site.

2. **PHPUnit**: PHPUnit is a popular testing framework for PHP that can be used with Drupal. PHPUnit provides a rich set of

tools and features for testing PHP code, including support for mock objects, data providers, and code coverage analysis.

3. **Behat**: Behat is a testing framework that allows you to write automated tests in plain English. With Behat, you can write tests that describe how your site should behave, and then run those tests to ensure that your site works as expected.

4. **Selenium**: Selenium is a browser automation tool that can be used to test Drupal sites. With Selenium, you can write tests that simulate user interactions with your site, such as clicking links and filling out forms.

5. **Testing in Drupal core:** Drupal core includes several testing modules that can be used to test core functionality, such as the Simpletest module and the PHPUnit module. These modules provide a good starting point for testing your code, and can help you ensure that your code works with the latest version of Drupal.

By using these tools and techniques, you can more easily test your Drupal code and identify and fix issues quickly.

5.4.13. Version Control with Git and GitHub

Version control is an essential part of software development, and Git is one of the most popular version control systems available. Git is a distributed version control system that allows you to track changes to your code over time, collaborate with others, and revert to previous versions if necessary.

GitHub is a web-based platform that provides hosting for Git repositories. It allows you to easily collaborate with others, manage issues and pull requests, and automate workflows using GitHub Actions.

Here are some basic steps for using Git and GitHub with your Drupal project:

1. Create a new Git repository: To create a new Git repository, navigate to the root directory of your Drupal project and run the command git init.
2. Create a new GitHub repository: To create a new GitHub repository, navigate to the GitHub website and click on the "New" button. Follow the instructions to create a new repository and link it to your local Git repository.
3. Add and commit changes: Once you have made changes to your Drupal project, you can add and commit those changes to your local Git repository using the commands git add . and git commit -m "commit message".
4. Push changes to GitHub: To push your changes to the GitHub repository, use the command git push.
5. Collaborate with others: With Git and GitHub, you can easily collaborate with others by creating branches, opening pull requests, and reviewing and merging changes.

Using version control with Git and GitHub can help you to better manage your Drupal project, collaborate with others, and maintain a history of your code changes over time.

5.4.14. GitLab and Deploying

GitLab is a web-based Git repository manager that provides version control, continuous integration, and continuous deployment functionalities. It is a great alternative to other Git hosting services like GitHub and Bitbucket, as it offers unlimited private repositories, built-in CI/CD, and other useful features.

When it comes to deploying Drupal 10, GitLab can be a valuable tool as it allows you to automate the deployment process and ensure consistency across your environments. Here are the basic steps for setting up GitLab for deployment:

1. Create a new repository in GitLab for your Drupal 10 site.
2. Clone the repository to your local machine.
3. Create a .gitlab-ci.yml file in the root of your Drupal 10 site, which defines the jobs that will be executed during the CI/CD process.
4. Define the stages of the deployment process. For example, you may have a "build" stage for compiling and packaging your code, a "test" stage for running automated tests, and a "deploy" stage for deploying your code to a production environment.
5. Use GitLab's built-in CI/CD features to automate the deployment process. For example, you can configure GitLab to automatically deploy your code to a staging environment whenever you push changes to a certain branch, or to deploy to a production environment after passing all tests in the CI/CD pipeline.
6. Once you have configured the CI/CD pipeline, you can use GitLab's deployment tools to manage your environments. For example, you can use GitLab's "environments" feature to track the status of your different environments, and to roll back to a previous version if needed.

Overall, GitLab can be a powerful tool for managing your Drupal 10 deployments, and can help you automate the deployment process while maintaining consistency and reliability across your environments.

5.4.15. GitHub Copilot and AI

GitHub Copilot is an AI-powered code completion tool that uses machine learning models to suggest code as you write it. It was created by OpenAI and GitHub, and is available as a plugin for Visual Studio Code.

Using natural language input and context from your codebase, GitHub Copilot generates suggestions for completing code, including entire functions, based on patterns it has learned from existing code. It can even generate code that is not present in your codebase, but is commonly used in other similar projects.

While GitHub Copilot can be a useful tool for developers looking to speed up their coding process, it is important to keep in mind that the code generated by the tool should always be reviewed and tested thoroughly. As with any AI tool, there is a risk of bias and errors, and it is up to the developer to ensure the quality and security of the code.

To use GitHub Copilot, you need to have a GitHub account and install the Visual Studio Code plugin. Once installed, you can activate Copilot by typing a trigger phrase and providing some context for the code you are trying to write. Copilot will then generate suggestions for you to choose from.

Overall, GitHub Copilot is an exciting development in the world of coding tools, and has the potential to significantly speed up the coding process for developers. However, as with any tool, it is important to use it responsibly and with caution.

5.4.16. Module filestructure

A Drupal module consists of several files and folders that define the functionality and behavior of the module. The root folder of a module typically has the same name as the module, and it is located in the modules folder of a Drupal site. Here's a breakdown of the most important files and folders in a Drupal module:

1. module_name.info.yml - This file contains information about the module, such as the module name, description, version, dependencies, and other metadata. It is a required file for all Drupal modules.

2. module_name.module - This file contains the code that implements the module's functionality. It may contain hook implementations, custom functions, and other code that interacts with Drupal's APIs.

3. module_name.routing.yml - This file defines the URLs (routes) that the module provides, and maps them to specific controller functions or callbacks.

4. module_name.links.menu.yml - This file defines the module's menu links, which are used to provide navigation to the module's pages.

5. module_name.links.action.yml - This file defines the module's actions, which are used to provide context-sensitive actions for the module's pages.

6. src/ - This folder contains the module's PHP classes, such as controllers, plugins, forms, and services. It is only required for modules that define custom classes.

7. templates/ - This folder contains the module's Twig templates, which are used to render HTML output for the module's pages.
8. config/install/ - This folder contains the module's default configuration files, which are used to configure the module when it is installed.
9. config/schema/ - This folder contains the module's schema files, which define the structure of the module's configuration data.
10. tests/ - This folder contains the module's PHPUnit tests, which are used to test the module's functionality.

The exact file structure of a Drupal module may vary depending on the specific requirements of the module, but the files and folders listed above are the most common and important ones.

5.4.17 Controllers in a Module

In this chapter, we will dive into creating custom controllers within a module in Drupal 10. Controllers are an essential part of the Drupal ecosystem, handling the business logic and returning the response for a specific route. By the end of this chapter, you will have a solid understanding of how to create and use controllers in your custom module.

Understanding Controllers

Controllers are classes responsible for handling incoming HTTP requests in a Drupal application. They define methods that correspond to specific routes and return responses, such as HTML or JSON. In Drupal, controllers are a fundamental part of the routing system, which maps URLs to the corresponding code that should be executed when that URL is accessed.

Creating a Custom Controller

To create a custom controller, follow these steps:

1. Create a new folder called src/Controller within your module's directory.
2. Create a new PHP file with the desired controller class name, such as MyController.php.
3. Inside this file, define a namespace for your controller class. The namespace should follow the format Drupal\<module_name>\Controller.
4. Import the necessary classes and interfaces at the beginning of your file, such as use Drupal\Core\Controller\ControllerBase;.
5. Define your controller class, which should extend ControllerBase.
6. Implement the desired methods within your controller class, following the pattern public function methodName(). These methods will represent the different routes that your controller will handle.

Registering Routes

To map a URL to a controller method, you must define a route in your module's my_module.routing.yml file. This file should be located at the root of your module's directory. Each route definition should have a unique route name, a path, and a reference to the corresponding controller method.

Accessing Services and Parameters

To access Drupal services and parameters in your controller, you can use dependency injection. Implement the ContainerInjectionInterface and define a create method that receives the necessary services or parameters from the container. Then, store the services or parameters in your controller class properties for further use.

1. Controllers in Drupal: A controller is a PHP class that handles incoming requests and generates responses for a Drupal module. Controllers are responsible for handling requests and producing responses, and they are often used to generate HTML or other types of content.

2. Defining a Controller: In order to define a controller in a Drupal module, you'll need to create a new PHP class that extends the ControllerBase class. This class will contain methods that handle incoming requests and generate responses.

3. Routing: In order for a controller to be able to handle incoming requests, you'll need to define a route that maps the request to the controller method. This is done using the routing system in Drupal, which allows you to define URLs and map them to specific controllers.

4. Access Control: Drupal's access control system allows you to restrict access to certain routes and controller methods based on a user's role or permissions. This can be done using the access callback and access arguments properties in your route definition.
5. Dependency Injection: Dependency injection is a technique that allows you to inject dependencies into your controller class, rather than hard-coding them. This can make your code more modular and easier to test.
6. Rendering Responses: Controllers are responsible for rendering responses to incoming requests. In Drupal, this is typically done using render arrays, which allow you to define the structure and content of your response.
7. Return Types: In addition to render arrays, controllers can also return other types of responses, such as HTTP redirect responses or JSON data.

5.4.17.1 Introduction: Controllers and the MVC Design Pattern

In the context of web development, the Model-View-Controller (MVC) design pattern is a popular way of organizing code. This pattern separates the concerns of data (the model), presentation (the view), and user interaction (the controller) into distinct components, making it easier to manage and maintain complex applications.

A controller is a component that handles incoming requests and coordinates the flow of data between the model and the view. In Drupal, controllers are used to build pages and other responses to user requests. They receive input data, process it, and return a response that can be displayed in the user's browser.

Drupal 8 introduced a new way of creating controllers, using the Symfony framework. This means that developers who are familiar with Symfony can leverage their existing knowledge to create custom Drupal controllers.

In the next sections, we'll take a closer look at how controllers work in Drupal, and how you can use them to build custom functionality for your site.

5.4.17.2 Drupal Controllers

In Drupal, controllers are PHP classes that are responsible for handling requests and generating responses. They are a fundamental part of the Drupal core system and are used extensively in the creation of custom modules.

When a request is made to a Drupal site, the routing system determines which controller should handle the request based on the URL and the associated route definition. The controller then processes the request and returns a response, which can be HTML, JSON, or any other format.

5.4.17.3 Using Controllers in Custom Modules

To use controllers in a custom module, you first need to define a route that maps a URL pattern to a controller method. This can be done using the routing.yml file in your module's root directory.

Once you have defined the route, you can create a controller class that implements the logic for the route. The controller should extend the ControllerBase class and define a method that corresponds to the route definition. This method should return a Response object that contains the output for the request.

Here's an example of a simple controller class that returns a message when the route is accessed:

```php
<?php

namespace Drupal\my_module\Controller;

use Drupal\Core\Controller\ControllerBase;
use Symfony\Component\HttpFoundation\Response;

/**
 * Controller for the hello route.
 */
class HelloController extends ControllerBase {

  /**
   * Returns a greeting message.
   */
  public function hello() {
    $message = 'Hello, world!';
    return new Response($message);
  }

}
```

To make this controller available to Drupal, you need to register it as a service in your module's .services.yml file. This can be done using the controller.service_arguments tag, like so:

```
services:
  my_module.hello_controller:
    class: Drupal\my_module\Controller\HelloController
    tags:
      - { name: controller.service_arguments }
```

With the controller class and route defined, you can now access the route and see the output of the hello() method by visiting the corresponding URL.

Controllers are a powerful tool for building custom functionality in Drupal, and can be used to handle a wide range of requests and responses. With a solid understanding of how they work, you can take your Drupal development skills to the next level and create truly custom, dynamic websites.

5.4.17.4 Routing in Drupal 10

Routing in Drupal 10 is the process of mapping incoming requests to their corresponding controllers. This is done through the use of routing YAML files, which define the URL patterns and associated controllers for your module's functionality.

The routing system in Drupal is built on top of the Symfony Routing component, which provides a powerful and flexible way to define URL patterns and their associated actions.

To define a route in Drupal 10, you need to create a YAML file in your module's routing directory. The file should be named with the pattern {module_name}.routing.yml. For example, if your module is named my_module, the routing file should be named my_module.routing.yml.

Here's an example of a basic routing definition in Drupal 10:

```
my_module.page:
  path: '/my-page'
  defaults:
   _controller:
'\Drupal\my_module\Controller\MyController::myPage'
   _title: 'My Page'
  requirements:
   _permission: 'access content'
```

In this example, we're defining a route with the name my_module.page, which maps to the URL /my-page. The defaults section defines the controller that should be called when this route is accessed, as well as the title of the page. The requirements section specifies any additional requirements for accessing the page, such as a required permission.

In addition to defining basic routes, Drupal 10 also provides a number of more advanced routing features, such as:

- Route parameters: This allows you to define dynamic parts of a URL, such as IDs or slugs, and pass them to your controller as arguments.
- Route options: This provides additional configuration options for your routes, such as setting a custom cache tag or defining a fallback controller.

- Route collections: This allows you to group related routes together and apply common configuration options to them.

By using these advanced routing features, you can build complex and flexible URL patterns that are tailored to the specific needs of your module.

Overall, routing is a critical component of building custom functionality in Drupal 10, and mastering its concepts and features is essential for any developer looking to build powerful and flexible modules.

5.4.17.5 Best Practices for Controllers in Drupal 10

When building controllers in Drupal 10, it's important to follow best practices to ensure that your code is maintainable, scalable, and efficient. Here are some tips to keep in mind:

1. Use Dependency Injection: Controllers should never instantiate services or dependencies directly. Instead, they should use dependency injection to receive these objects from the service container. This makes your code more modular and testable, and allows you to easily swap out dependencies if needed.
2. Keep Controllers Small and Focused: Controllers should have a single responsibility, and should be kept as small and focused as possible. This makes your code more maintainable and easier to test, and helps to avoid spaghetti code.
3. Use Annotations to Define Routes: In Drupal 10, routes can be defined using annotations in the controller class. This makes it easy to define routes and keep them

organized, and allows you to take advantage of features like path aliases, argument conversion, and more.

4. Use Typed Parameters: In Drupal 10, you can use type-hinted parameters in your controller methods to automatically receive arguments from the route. This makes your code more readable and self-documenting, and ensures that your code is type-safe.

5. Use the Right Response Type: Controllers should return the appropriate response type based on the content they are returning. For example, if your controller is returning HTML, you should use the HtmlResponse class, while if you are returning JSON, you should use the JsonResponse class. This ensures that your code is efficient and consistent, and helps to avoid issues with cross-site scripting (XSS) attacks.

By following these best practices, you can ensure that your controllers are well-organized, maintainable, and scalable, and that your Drupal 10 site is built to the highest standards.

5.4.17.6 Controllers as a Fundamental Building Block

Controllers are a fundamental building block of Drupal 10 modules, enabling developers to define custom URL routes and handle user requests. They are an essential part of building custom functionality for Drupal sites, and understanding how they work is crucial for anyone looking to develop modules for the platform.

By following best practices for creating controllers, such as separating concerns and keeping code organized, developers can create modular, maintainable code that can be easily extended and reused in other projects. With the power of controllers and other key Drupal concepts like the MVC design pattern and routing, developers have the tools they need to create custom functionality that can take their sites to the next level.

While working with controllers can seem daunting at first, taking the time to learn and understand them is well worth the effort. Whether you're a seasoned Drupal developer or just getting started, controllers are an essential tool to have in your toolkit, enabling you to build powerful, flexible, and scalable custom functionality for Drupal 10 sites.

5.4.17.7: Dependency Injection in Controllers

Dependency Injection (DI) is a design pattern that allows for the decoupling of components, making them more modular, testable, and maintainable. In this section, we will discuss how to use Dependency Injection in your custom Drupal controllers, enabling you to access and utilize various services and parameters from the Drupal service container.

5.4.17.7.1: Understanding Dependency Injection

Dependency Injection involves providing an object with the dependencies (services or parameters) it requires, rather than having the object create or look for those dependencies itself. By injecting dependencies into your controllers, you can improve the testability and maintainability of your code. Drupal's service container manages the instantiation and sharing of services throughout the application, making it easy to inject dependencies into your custom controllers.

5.4.17.7.2: Implementing Dependency Injection in Controllers

To use Dependency Injection in your custom controllers, follow these steps:

1. Import the necessary classes and interfaces at the beginning of your controller file, such as use Drupal\Core\DependencyInjection\ContainerInjectionInterface; and use Symfony\Component\DependencyInjection\ContainerInterface;.

2. Have your controller class implement the ContainerInjectionInterface:

```
class MyController extends ControllerBase
implements ContainerInjectionInterface {
  // ...
}
```

3. Define a constructor for your controller class that receives the necessary dependencies as arguments. Store the dependencies as class properties for later use:

```
protected $myService;
```

```php
public function __construct(MyServiceInterface
$my_service) {
  $this->myService = $my_service;
}
```

4. Implement the create method, which is part of the
ContainerInjectionInterface. This method should
receive a ContainerInterface object, which you can use
to get the required services or parameters. Then,
instantiate and return a new instance of your controller,
passing the retrieved dependencies as arguments to the
constructor:

```php
<?php

namespace Drupal\my_module\Controller;

use Drupal\Core\Controller\ControllerBase;
use
Drupal\Core\DependencyInjection\ContainerInjectionInterf
ace;
use Drupal\Core\Session\AccountInterface;
use
Symfony\Component\DependencyInjection\ContainerInterf
ace;

class MyController extends ControllerBase
implements ContainerInjectionInterface {

  protected $currentUser;
```

```php
public function __construct(AccountInterface $current_user) {
  $this->currentUser = $current_user;
}

public static function create(ContainerInterface $container) {
  return new static(
    $container->get('current_user')
  );
}

public function content() {
  $user_name = $this->currentUser->getDisplayName();
  return [
    '#type' => 'markup',
    '#markup' => $this->t('Hello, @name!', ['@name' =>
$user_name]),
  ];
}

}
```

Here's an example of a complete custom controller that uses Dependency Injection to access the current_user service:

```php
<?php

namespace Drupal\my_module\Controller;

use Drupal\Core\Controller\ControllerBase;
use
```

```php
Drupal\Core\DependencyInjection\ContainerInjectionInterface
;
use Drupal\Core\Session\AccountInterface;
use
Symfony\Component\DependencyInjection\ContainerInterfac
e;

class MyController extends ControllerBase
 implements ContainerInjectionInterface {

  protected $currentUser;

  public function __construct(AccountInterface $current_user) {
    $this->currentUser = $current_user;
  }

  public static function create(ContainerInterface $container) {
    return new static(
      $container->get('current_user')
    );
  }

  public function content() {
    $user_name = $this->currentUser->getDisplayName();
    return [
     '#type' => 'markup',
     '#markup' => $this->t('Hello, @name!', ['@name' =>
$user_name]),
    ];
  }
}
```

By using Dependency Injection in your custom controllers, you can take advantage of Drupal's powerful service container and improve the overall quality and maintainability of your code.

5.4.18: Creating Services in a Drupal 10 Module

Services in Drupal are reusable components that perform specific tasks or encapsulate a particular functionality. They are managed by the Drupal service container, which ensures efficient handling of dependencies and object instantiation. In this chapter, we will explore how to create and utilize custom services in a Drupal 10 module.

5.4.18.1: Understanding Services

Services in Drupal are objects that are instantiated and managed by the Drupal service container. They are designed to be reusable, allowing you to access the same functionality across different components of your application. By encapsulating specific functionalities into services, you can improve the modularity and maintainability of your code.

5.4.18.2: Creating a Custom Service

To create a custom service, follow these steps:

1. Create a new folder called src within your module's directory, if it does not already exist.

2. Inside the src folder, create another folder called Service.
3. Create a new PHP file with the desired service class name, such as MyService.php.
4. Define a namespace for your service class. The namespace should follow the format Drupal\<module_name>\Service.
5. Import any necessary classes and interfaces at the beginning of your file.
6. Define your service class with the desired functionality.

Here's an example of a simple custom service:

```php
<?php

namespace Drupal\my_module\Service;

class MyService {

  public function getMessage() {
    return 'Hello from MyService!';
  }
}
```

5.4.18.3: Registering the Service

To make your custom service available to the Drupal service container, you must register it in your module's my_module.services.yml file. This file should be located at the root of your module's directory. Each service definition should have a unique service ID and a reference to the corresponding service class.

Here's an example service definition:

```
services:
  my_module.my_service:
    class: Drupal\my_module\Service\MyService
```

5.4.18.4: Using the Service in Your Module

Once your custom service is registered with the Drupal service container, you can access it in your module using Dependency Injection. For example, to use your custom service in a controller, you would inject it as a dependency by implementing the ContainerInjectionInterface and following the Dependency Injection steps explained in the previous chapter (5.4.17.7).

Here's an example of a controller that uses the custom MyService:

```
<?php

namespace Drupal\my_module\Controller;

use Drupal\Core\Controller\ControllerBase;
use
Drupal\Core\DependencyInjection\ContainerInjectionInterf
```

```
ace;
use Drupal\my_module\Service\MyService;
use
Symfony\Component\DependencyInjection\ContainerInterf
ace;

class MyController extends ControllerBase
implements ContainerInjectionInterface {

  protected $myService;

  public function __construct(MyService $my_service) {
    $this->myService = $my_service;
  }

  public static function create(ContainerInterface
$container) {
    return new static(
      $container->get('my_module.my_service')
    );
  }

  public function content() {
    $message = $this->myService->getMessage();
    return [
      '#type' => 'markup',
      '#markup' => $this->t('@message', ['@message' =>
$message]),
    ];
  }

}
```

In conclusion, services are an essential part of building maintainable and modular Drupal applications. By creating custom services in your Drupal 10 module, you can encapsulate specific functionalities and reuse them across your application.

5.4.19: Creating Forms in a Drupal 10 Module

Forms are a fundamental aspect of web applications, allowing users to input data and interact with the system. In this chapter, we will discuss how to create custom forms in a Drupal 10 module, leveraging Drupal's powerful Form API to build flexible and secure forms.

5.4.19.1: Understanding Drupal's Form API

Drupal's Form API provides a robust and flexible framework for creating, validating, and processing forms in Drupal applications. It offers a declarative approach to building forms, abstracting away the complexities of HTML and JavaScript while ensuring security and accessibility best practices.

5.4.19.2: Creating a Custom Form

To create a custom form, follow these steps:

1. Create a new folder called src/Form within your module's directory.

2. Create a new PHP file with the desired form class name, such as MyForm.php.

3. Define a namespace for your form class. The namespace should follow the format Drupal\<module_name>\Form.

4. Import any necessary classes and interfaces at the beginning of your file, such as use Drupal\Core\Form\FormBase; and use Drupal\Core\Form\FormStateInterface;.

5. Define your form class, which should extend FormBase.

6. Implement the required methods within your form class, such as getFormId(), buildForm(), and submitForm().

Here's an example of a simple custom form:

```php
<?php
```

```php
namespace Drupal\my_module\Form;

use Drupal\Core\Form\FormBase;
use Drupal\Core\Form\FormStateInterface;

class MyForm extends FormBase {

  public function getFormId() {
    return 'my_module_my_form';
  }

  public function buildForm(array $form,
FormStateInterface $form_state) {
    $form['name'] = [
      '#type' => 'textfield',
      '#title' => $this->t('Name'),
      '#required' => TRUE,
    ];

    $form['submit'] = [
      '#type' => 'submit',
      '#value' => $this->t('Submit'),
    ];

    return $form;
  }

  public function submitForm(array &$form,
FormStateInterface $form_state) {
    drupal_set_message($this->t('Hello, @name!',
['@name' => $form_state->getValue('name')]));
```

```
    }
}
```

5.4.19.3: Displaying the Form

To display your custom form, you can create a route and controller that returns the form as a renderable array. In your controller, use the createForm() method provided by the ControllerBase class to create an instance of your form and return it.

Here's an example controller that displays the MyForm:

```php
<?php

namespace Drupal\my_module\Controller;

use Drupal\Core\Controller\ControllerBase;
use Drupal\my_module\Form\MyForm;
```

```
class MyController extends ControllerBase {

  public function content() {
    $form = $this->createForm(MyForm::class);
    return $form;
  }

}
```

5.4.19.4: Form Validation

Here's an example of a custom form with validation:

```
public function validateForm(array &$form,
  FormStateInterface $form_state) {
  $name = $form_state->getValue('name');
  if (strlen($name) < 3) {
    $form_state->setError($form['name'],
    $this->t('The name must be at least 3 characters long.'));
  }
}
```

In the example above, the validateForm() method checks if the

name field's value is at least 3 characters long. If it isn't, an error

is added to the field using the $form_state->setError() method.

The error message will be displayed next to the field when the form is submitted.

5.4.19.5: Ajax-enabled Forms

To add Ajax functionality to your custom form, you can leverage Drupal's built-in Ajax API. You can define Ajax callbacks for your form elements, which are automatically triggered when the element changes or is submitted.

Here's an example of a custom form with Ajax functionality:

```
use Drupal\Core\Ajax\AjaxResponse;
use Drupal\Core\Ajax\HtmlCommand;

public function buildForm(array $form,
  FormStateInterface $form_state) {
  $form['name'] = [
    '#type' => 'textfield',
    '#title' => $this->t('Name'),
    '#required' => TRUE,
    '#ajax' => [
      'callback' => '::ajaxResponse',
      'wrapper' => 'name-message',
      'event' => 'change',
    ],
  ];
```

```
$form['name_message'] = [
  '#type' => 'html_tag',
  '#tag' => 'div',
  '#attributes' => ['id' => 'name-message'],
];

$form['submit'] = [
  '#type' => 'submit',
  '#value' => $this->t('Submit'),
];

return $form;
}

public function ajaxResponse(array &$form,
FormStateInterface $form_state) {
  $response = new AjaxResponse();
  $message = $this->t('Hello, @name!',
  ['@name' => $form_state->getValue('name')]);
  $response->addCommand(new
HtmlCommand('#name-message',
  $message));

  return $response;
}
```

In this example, we've added an Ajax callback to the name field

using the #ajax property. The callback method ajaxResponse()

is responsible for generating the Ajax response, which updates the contents of the name-message wrapper element.

In conclusion, Drupal's Form API provides a powerful and flexible framework for creating custom forms in your Drupal 10 module. By leveraging the API's features, you can build secure, accessible, and feature-rich forms to enhance your application's functionality.

Chapter 5.4.20: Creating Plugins in a Drupal 10 Module

Introduction

Drupal's plugin system allows developers to create reusable and extensible functionality that can be utilized by other components within the system. In this chapter, we will discuss how to create custom plugins in a Drupal 10 module, which can be used to enhance various aspects of your application.

5.4.20.1: Understanding Drupal's Plugin System

Drupal's plugin system is a flexible and extensible way to create functionality that can be discovered and used by other parts of the system. Plugins can be used to provide functionality for various subsystems, such as blocks, field formatters, and views.

A plugin consists of the following components:

1. A plugin type, which defines the overall structure and requirements for the plugins of that type.
2. A plugin manager, which is responsible for discovering, instantiating, and managing plugins of a specific type.
3. Plugin implementations, which are individual instances of a plugin that provide the desired functionality.

5.4.20.2: Creating a Custom Plugin

To create a custom plugin, follow these steps:

1. Choose or create a plugin type for your plugin. If you want to extend an existing subsystem like blocks or

field formatters, you can use the corresponding plugin type. If you need to create a new plugin type, you will need to define a plugin manager and an interface for your plugin type.

2. Create a new folder within your module's src/Plugin directory that corresponds to your plugin type. For example, if you are creating a custom block plugin, the folder should be named Block.

3. Create a new PHP file with the desired plugin class name, such as MyPlugin.php.

4. Define a namespace for your plugin class. The namespace should follow the format Drupal\<module_name>\Plugin\<plugin_type>.

5. Import any necessary classes and interfaces at the beginning of your file.

6. Define your plugin class, which should extend the appropriate base class or implement the required interface for your plugin type.

7. Provide the necessary annotations to define your plugin's metadata, such as its ID, label, and other properties.

Here's an example of a simple custom block plugin:

```php
<?php

namespace Drupal\my_module\Plugin\Block;

use Drupal\Core\Block\BlockBase;

/**
 * Provides a 'MyPlugin' block.
 *
 * @Block(
 *   id = "my_plugin",
 *   admin_label = @Translation("My Plugin"),
 * )
 */
class MyPlugin extends BlockBase {

  public function build() {
    return [
      '#type' => 'markup',
      '#markup' => $this->t('Hello from My Plugin!'),
    ];
  }

}
```

5.4.20.3: Using the Plugin

Once your custom plugin is created, it can be discovered and used by the corresponding subsystem. For example, a custom block plugin will be available in the block layout administration page, where it can be placed in a region and configured.

If you have created a new plugin type, you can use your plugin manager to discover and instantiate plugins of that type within your application.

In conclusion, Drupal's plugin system provides a powerful and flexible way to create reusable and extensible functionality in your Drupal 10 module. By creating custom plugins, you can enhance various aspects of your application and provide a modular and maintainable codebase.

5.4.20: Patching a Module in Drupal 10

There may be times when you need to apply a patch to a module in Drupal, either to fix a bug, implement a new feature, or modify the module to meet your specific requirements. In this chapter, we will discuss how to patch a module in Drupal 10, including finding existing patches, creating your own patch, and applying the patch using the Composer workflow.

5.4.20.1: Finding Existing Patches

Before creating a patch, it is important to check whether a similar patch has already been created by someone else. You can search for existing patches in the following locations:

1. Drupal.org: Search the module's issue queue on Drupal.org to see if there is an existing patch related to the issue you are trying to fix or the feature you want to implement.

2. Drupal contributed modules: Some modules may include patches for other modules in their documentation or in a patches directory within the module.

3. Community resources: Check community forums, blog posts, and other online resources related to the module, as someone may have shared a patch for a similar issue.

5.4.20.2: Creating Your Own Patch

If you cannot find an existing patch, you can create your own. To create a patch, follow these steps:

1. Clone the module's repository to your local environment.
2. Create a new branch for your changes using a descriptive name, such as fix-bug-12345 or add-feature-xyz.
3. Make the necessary changes to the module's codebase.
4. Commit your changes with a descriptive commit message that explains the changes you made and their purpose.
5. Create a patch file by generating a diff between your branch and the original branch. You can use the git diff command or a graphical diff tool to create the patch file. Ensure that the patch file has a .patch extension and follows the naming convention: [module_name]-[short_description]-[issue_number]-[comment_number].patch.

5.4.20.3: Applying the Patch with Composer

To apply a patch to a module using Composer, follow these steps:

1. Ensure that the patch file is accessible online, either by uploading it to a public server or by referencing a patch file from a publicly accessible repository, such as an issue on Drupal.org.

2. Add the patch to your project's composer.json file in the extra section. The patch should be listed under the patches key, with the module name as the key and the patch URL as the value.

Here's an example of how to add a patch in the composer.json file:

```
{
  "extra": {
    "patches": {
      "drupal/module_name": {
        "Short description of the patch":
```

```
          "https://example.com/path/to/your/patch-file.patch"
  }
    }
      }
        }
```

3. Run composer install or composer update to apply the patch to the module. Composer will download the patch and apply it to the specified module. If the patch is successfully applied, you will see a message indicating the successful application of the patch.

4. Test the patched module to ensure that it works as expected and does not introduce new issues.

5.4.20.4: Updating a Patched Module

When updating a module with a patch applied, it is important to ensure that the patch is still compatible with the new version of the module. You may need to update the patch, create a new patch, or remove the patch if the new module version has incorporated the changes from the patch.

In conclusion, patching a module in Drupal 10 allows you to fix issues, implement new features, or modify the module to meet your specific requirements. By using the Composer workflow to apply patches, you can maintain a consistent and manageable codebase while ensuring that your customizations are preserved during updates. Remember to always test your patched modules to ensure compatibility and stability, and contribute your patches back to the community if they can be helpful to others.

5.5: Most Popular and Common Drupal Modules

This chapter provides a list of some of the most popular and commonly used modules in the Drupal ecosystem. These modules have been widely adopted by the Drupal community due to their functionality, flexibility, and ease of use. By familiarizing yourself with these modules, you can enhance your Drupal site and save development time.

1. Views (https://www.drupal.org/project/views)

Views is a powerful module that allows you to create, manage, and display dynamic lists of content based on various criteria, such as content type, tags, or date. With a user-friendly UI, you can quickly build complex content displays without writing any code.

2. Pathauto
(https://www.drupal.org/project/pathauto)

Pathauto automatically generates URL aliases for your content, based on configurable patterns. This module helps improve the SEO and readability of your site's URLs.

3. Token (https://www.drupal.org/project/token)

Token provides a centralized API for using placeholders (tokens) in text. It is often used in conjunction with other modules, such as Pathauto, to create dynamic URL aliases or other text-based configurations.

4. Chaos Tool Suite (ctools)
(https://www.drupal.org/project/ctools)

Chaos Tool Suite (ctools) is a set of APIs and tools that helps module developers create advanced functionality more efficiently. It is a dependency for several other popular modules, such as Views and Panels.

5. Webform
   (https://www.drupal.org/project/webform)

Webform is a powerful module for creating and managing forms, surveys, and quizzes on your Drupal site. It provides a user-friendly interface to design forms, track submissions, and export data.

6. Metatag
   (https://www.drupal.org/project/metatag)

Metatag allows you to manage meta tags for your site's pages, helping you improve SEO and control how your content is displayed when shared on social media platforms.

7. Paragraphs
   (https://www.drupal.org/project/paragraphs)

Paragraphs is a flexible and user-friendly module that enables content creators to build rich, structured content using pre-defined components. It provides an alternative to traditional, monolithic body fields by allowing you to create complex layouts and nested content structures.

8. Entity Reference
(https://www.drupal.org/project/entity_referenc
e)

Entity Reference is a field module that allows you to create relationships between different types of entities, such as nodes, users, and taxonomy terms. This module is useful for creating related content, author attribution, or organizing content hierarchies.

9. Search API
(https://www.drupal.org/project/search_api)

Search API is a flexible, extensible framework for creating custom search experiences on your Drupal site. It supports various backends, such as database or Apache Solr, and integrates with other modules to provide advanced search features like faceted search and full-text search.

10. Redirect
(https://www.drupal.org/project/redirect)

Redirect is a module that helps you manage URL redirections on your site. It allows you to create and track 301 and 302 redirects, ensuring that your site maintains its SEO value and visitors can find your content.

11. Admin Toolbar

(https://www.drupal.org/project/admin_toolbar)

Admin Toolbar improves the default Drupal administration menu by providing a dropdown interface with quick access to administrative pages. This module enhances the usability and navigation of the admin interface, making it easier to manage your site.

12. Simple XML Sitemap

(https://www.drupal.org/project/simple_sitemap)

Simple XML Sitemap generates XML sitemaps for your Drupal site, which helps search engines crawl and index your content more efficiently. The module supports various Drupal entities, including nodes, taxonomy terms, and custom URLs.

13. Backup and Migrate
    (https://www.drupal.org/project/backup_migrat
    e)

Backup and Migrate is a module that simplifies the process of backing up and restoring your Drupal site. It allows you to create and manage backups of your site's database and files, as well as migrate your site between environments.

14. Field Group
    (https://www.drupal.org/project/field_group)

Field Group is a module that allows you to group fields together in your content types and display them in various formats, such as vertical tabs, accordions, or fieldsets. This module helps you create cleaner, more organized content editing forms.

15. Google Analytics
    (https://www.drupal.org/project/google_analyti
    cs)

Google Analytics is a module that integrates your Drupal site with the Google Analytics platform. It allows you to track user interactions, pageviews, and other metrics, providing valuable insights into your site's performance and user behavior.

16. Drupal Commerce (https://www.drupal.org/project/commerce)

Drupal Commerce is a powerful e-commerce module that provides a framework for creating online stores and managing products, orders, and payments. It is highly extensible and integrates with other Drupal modules to create a seamless shopping experience for your users.

17. Devel (https://www.drupal.org/project/devel)

Devel is a suite of developer tools and utilities that help you debug, analyze, and optimize your Drupal site. Some features include a query log, a variable inspector, and performance profiling.

18. Honeypot (https://www.drupal.org/project/honeypot)

Honeypot is an anti-spam module that helps protect your site from spam bots by using a hidden form field. This module is a lightweight and effective solution for reducing spam on your site without impacting user experience.

19. CKEditor (https://www.drupal.org/project/ckeditor)

CKEditor is a popular WYSIWYG (What You See Is What You Get) editor for Drupal that provides a rich text editing experience for content creators. It includes various features such as image uploading, text formatting, and HTML source editing.

20. Better Exposed Filters (https://www.drupal.org/project/better_exposed_filters)

Better Exposed Filters enhances the exposed filters functionality of Views, providing more customization options and improved usability. This module allows you to create more user-friendly and interactive filters for your content listings.

21. SMTP (https://www.drupal.org/project/smtp)

SMTP is a module that allows your Drupal site to send emails using an external SMTP server, ensuring more reliable email delivery. The module also provides a testing feature to verify that your SMTP settings are working correctly.

22. EU Cookie Compliance (https://www.drupal.org/project/eu_cookie_co mpliance)

EU Cookie Compliance is a module that helps your site comply with the European Union's cookie law by displaying a customizable cookie consent banner for site visitors.

23. Social Media Share (https://www.drupal.org/project/social_media_ share)

Social Media Share is a module that enables your users to share your site's content on various social media platforms, such as Facebook, Twitter, and LinkedIn. This module is customizable and supports multiple sharing widgets.

24. Block Class (https://www.drupal.org/project/block_class)

Block Class is a module that allows you to add custom CSS classes to your blocks, giving you more control over the styling and appearance of your site. This module is especially useful for themers and site builders who want to apply custom styles to specific blocks.

25. Libraries (https://www.drupal.org/project/libraries)

Libraries is a module that provides a centralized API for managing external libraries, such as JavaScript or CSS files, used by other modules or themes. This module ensures that your site loads the correct version of each library and avoids conflicts between different modules.

26. Scheduler (https://www.drupal.org/project/scheduler)

Scheduler is a module that enables you to schedule the publication and unpublishing of your content. This module is useful for managing time-sensitive content, such as news articles, promotions, or events.

27. Rules (https://www.drupal.org/project/rules)

Rules is a powerful module that allows you to create custom workflows and automate actions on your Drupal site. With Rules, you can create condition-based actions that trigger when specific events occur, such as sending an email when a new user registers or updating a field when content is published.

28. Linkit (https://www.drupal.org/project/linkit)

Linkit is a module that enhances the link creation experience in the CKEditor by providing an autocomplete search field for internal content. This module helps content creators easily create links to other nodes, users, or taxonomy terms without having to manually enter URLs.

29. Entity Browser (https://www.drupal.org/project/entity_browser)

Entity Browser is a module that provides a flexible and configurable interface for browsing and selecting entities, such as nodes, users, or media. This module can be integrated with other modules, like Entity Reference or Media, to create a more user-friendly content editing experience.

30. IMCE (https://www.drupal.org/project/imce)

IMCE is a file manager module that provides an easy-to-use interface for managing files and images on your Drupal site. It integrates with the CKEditor and other modules, allowing users to upload, browse, and insert images or files directly into their content.

31. Media Entity (https://www.drupal.org/project/media_entity)

Media Entity is a module that provides a base entity for handling different types of media, such as images, videos, or audio files. This module is the foundation for creating a flexible and extensible media management system in Drupal.

32. Group (https://www.drupal.org/project/group)

Group is a module that enables you to create and manage groups on your Drupal site, with each group having its content, members, and permissions. This module is useful for creating private areas, community features, or organizational structures within your site.

33. CAPTCHA (https://www.drupal.org/project/captcha)

CAPTCHA is a module that adds a challenge-response test to your forms to protect against spam submissions. The module supports various CAPTCHA types, such as image-based, mathematical, or question-based challenges.

34. Menu Block (https://www.drupal.org/project/menu_block)

Menu Block is a module that allows you to create custom menu blocks with specific menu levels, depth, and starting points. This module is useful for creating secondary or tertiary navigation structures, or for displaying parts of your menu hierarchy in different regions of your site.

35. Automatic Nodetitles (https://www.drupal.org/project/auto_nodetitle)

Automatic Nodetitles is a module that automatically generates the title field for nodes based on configurable patterns or token values. This module is useful for content types where the title is derived from other fields, such as dates, authors, or taxonomy terms.

36. Image Effects
(https://www.drupal.org/project/image_effects
)

Image Effects is a module that extends Drupal's core Image module by providing additional image effects, such as watermarking, text overlay, and color adjustments. This module helps you enhance and manipulate images on your site to create custom visuals and branding elements.

37. Workbench
(https://www.drupal.org/project/workbench)

Workbench is a suite of modules that provides a customizable editorial workflow and content management experience for Drupal. Key features include content moderation, access control, and content drafts. Workbench helps streamline the content creation and editing process, making it easier for teams to manage and collaborate on content.

38. Search API
(https://www.drupal.org/project/search_api)

Search API is a powerful and flexible module that provides a framework for creating custom search experiences on your

Drupal site. It supports various search backends, such as database or Solr, and allows you to create custom search indexes, facets, and filters.

39. Entityqueue
(https://www.drupal.org/project/entityqueue)

Entityqueue is a module that enables you to create custom ordered lists of entities, such as nodes or users. These ordered lists can be used for various purposes, such as featured content, slideshows, or curated lists. Entityqueue integrates with Views, making it easy to display and manage your ordered lists.

These popular and commonly used modules provide essential functionality for most Drupal sites. By leveraging these modules, you can enhance your site's features,
improve SEO, and streamline your content creation and management processes.

Chapter 6: Advanced Content Display

As your Drupal 10 site grows in complexity, you may need to display content in more advanced and customized ways to meet the diverse needs of your users. This chapter delves into various techniques and tools available for enhancing content display on your Drupal site, enabling you to create dynamic, responsive, and engaging user experiences.

In this chapter, we will explore various advanced content display strategies, including:

- Leveraging Views to create powerful and customizable content listings
- Enhancing content presentation using Display Suite and custom view modes
- Creating dynamic content layouts with the Layout Builder and layout plugins
- Incorporating third-party JavaScript libraries for advanced visual effects and interactivity
- Implementing responsive images and content to ensure optimal performance and user experience on all devices
- Personalizing content display based on user roles, preferences, or other contextual factors

By mastering these advanced content display techniques, you will be able to create visually appealing and engaging Drupal sites that cater to the unique needs of your audience and provide an exceptional user experience.

6.1. Views: Displaying Content Dynamically

Views is one of the most powerful and versatile tools in Drupal for creating dynamic content listings and displays. It is an essential component of any Drupal site and provides an easy-to-use interface for building and customizing content displays without writing any code. In this section, we will discuss how to create and configure Views to display content dynamically on your Drupal 10 site.

6.1.1: Creating a View

To create a new View, follow these steps:

1. Navigate to the Views administration page by clicking on 'Structure' in the admin toolbar, and then clicking on 'Views'.
2. Click the 'Add view' button to open the 'Add view' form.
3. Enter a name and description for your View.

4. Select the content type or entity type you want to display in the View.
5. Configure the display settings, such as the display format, items per page, and sorting options.
6. Choose whether to create a page, block, or other display type for the View, and configure the relevant settings, such as the path, menu item, or contextual filters.
7. Click the 'Save and edit' button to create the View and open the Views UI for further configuration.

6.1.2: Configuring the View

Once you have created a View, you can configure its various components to create a customized content display. Some of the key components you can configure in a View include:

1. Fields: Define which fields from the content or entity type you want to display, and configure their display settings, such as labels, formats, and rewriting options.
2. Filter criteria: Add filters to your View to limit the content displayed based on specific criteria, such as content type, published status, or taxonomy terms.
3. Sort criteria: Define how the content in your View should be sorted, either by specific fields or by properties such as creation date or author.
4. Relationships: Add relationships to your View to include related content or data from other entities, such as referencing or referenced entities, authors, or taxonomy terms.

5. Contextual filters: Use contextual filters to dynamically filter the content in your View based on contextual information, such as the current user, URL arguments, or other variables.

6.1.3: Display Types

Views supports multiple display types to suit different use cases. Some common display types include:

1. Page: Creates a standalone page with a URL path and optional menu item for your View.
2. Block: Generates a block that you can place in any region of your site.
3. Attachment: Allows you to attach the View to another View, either before or after the main content.
4. Feed: Creates an RSS or Atom feed for your View's content.

In conclusion, Views is a powerful and flexible tool for displaying content dynamically on your Drupal 10 site. By mastering the various components and settings available in Views, you can create a wide range of content displays, from simple lists to complex, contextually filtered displays, that cater to the unique needs of your audience.

6.2. Customizing View Displays and Filters

Customizing Views in Drupal 10 enables you to create highly tailored content displays that meet specific requirements and enhance the user experience. In this section, we will explore various techniques for customizing View displays and filters to create more advanced and dynamic content listings.

6.2.1: Display Modes

Display modes in Views allow you to define multiple variations of a single View, each with its own unique configuration. This can be useful for creating different content displays for different use cases or devices. To create a new display mode for a View, click the 'Add' button in the View's displays section and choose the desired display type.

6.2.2: Customizing Field Displays

Fields in Views can be customized to control their appearance, formatting, and behavior. Some options for customizing field displays include:

1. Labels: Control the visibility and appearance of field labels, either by hiding them or by specifying a custom label.

2. Formatter: Choose a field formatter to control how the field's value is displayed, such as plain text, HTML, or a custom formatter provided by a module.
3. Rewrite results: Modify the field's output by rewriting the value, combining fields, or adding custom HTML or tokens.

6.2.3: Advanced Filter Criteria

Filter criteria in Views can be customized to create complex and dynamic content filters. Some advanced filter criteria techniques include:

1. Exposed filters: Expose filters to users, allowing them to filter the content themselves based on the criteria you define.
2. Grouped filters: Combine multiple filter values into a single filter using the 'AND' or 'OR' operators, enabling you to create more complex filtering conditions.
3. Filter by field values: Filter content based on specific field values, such as filtering nodes by a taxonomy term or a custom field value.

6.2.4: Contextual Filters and Relationships

Contextual filters and relationships in Views enable you to create highly dynamic content displays that respond to the context in which they are used. Some examples of using contextual filters and relationships include:

1. Displaying related content: Use relationships to display content that is related to the current node or user, such as nodes that share the same author or have a common taxonomy term.
2. Filtering by URL arguments: Use contextual filters to filter content based on URL arguments, such as displaying all nodes of a specific content type or by a specific author.
3. Personalizing content displays: Create personalized content displays by filtering content based on the current user's roles, preferences, or other attributes.

In conclusion, customizing View displays and filters in Drupal 10 allows you to create highly tailored and dynamic content listings that cater to the unique needs of your audience. By leveraging the advanced configuration options available in Views, you can design content displays that are visually engaging, contextually relevant, and highly functional.

6.3. Integrating Views with Other Components

Integrating Views with other components and modules in Drupal 10 can greatly enhance the functionality and user experience of your content displays. In this section, we will explore various techniques for integrating Views with other components, such as blocks, menus, and third-party modules, to create more powerful and dynamic content displays.

6.3.1: Embedding Views in Blocks and Menus

Views can be integrated with blocks and menus to provide dynamic content displays in different areas of your site:

Blocks: Create a block display in your View to generate a block that can be placed in any region of your site. This can be useful for displaying featured content, recent news, or other dynamic content listings in sidebars or other areas outside the main content region.

Menus: Add a menu item for your View's page display to integrate it into your site's navigation. This can be useful for creating dynamic content listings that are easily accessible to users, such as a blog archive, product catalog, or event calendar.

6.3.2: Integrating Views with Taxonomy and Entity Reference

Views can be integrated with taxonomy and entity reference fields to create powerful content displays that leverage the relationships between content:

Taxonomy: Use relationships and contextual filters to create Views that display content tagged with specific taxonomy terms or term hierarchies. This can be useful for creating topic-based content listings, such as a blog archive organized by category or a product catalog organized by product type.

Entity reference: Use relationships to display content that is related to other content through entity reference fields, such as displaying a list of related articles, products, or events.

6.3.3: Integrating Views with Third-Party Modules

There are many third-party modules available that extend the functionality of Views and enable you to create more advanced and dynamic content displays:

Views Slideshow: A popular module that allows you to create responsive slideshows and carousels using your View's content.

Views Accordion: A module that enables you to display your View's content in an expandable accordion-style format.

Views Infinite Scroll: A module that adds infinite scrolling functionality to your Views, allowing users to load more content as they scroll down the page.

To integrate a third-party module with Views, install and enable the module, then configure the appropriate settings within the Views UI, such as adding a new display format or modifying existing display settings.

In conclusion, integrating Views with other components and modules in Drupal 10 enables you to create more powerful and dynamic content displays that enhance the user experience and functionality of your site. By leveraging the capabilities of blocks, menus, taxonomy, entity reference, and third-party modules, you can design content displays that are visually engaging, contextually relevant, and highly functional.

6.4. Display Suite and Panels

Display Suite and Panels are two powerful Drupal modules that allow you to create custom layouts and content displays without writing any code. In this section, we will explore how to use Display Suite and Panels to create advanced content displays and layouts for your Drupal 10 site.

6.4.1: Display Suite

Display Suite is a flexible module that enables you to create custom view modes and layouts for your content types, users, comments, and other entities. Some key features of Display Suite include:

1. Custom view modes: Create custom view modes for your entities, allowing you to define multiple display configurations for different use cases or contexts.
2. Custom layouts: Define custom layouts for your entities, either by using predefined layouts provided by Display Suite or by creating your own custom layouts using HTML and CSS.
3. Field display customization: Control the appearance and formatting of fields in your layouts, such as hiding labels, applying custom CSS classes, or modifying field output.

To get started with Display Suite, install and enable the module, then navigate to the 'Display modes' configuration page under 'Structure' in the admin toolbar. From there, you can create custom view modes and configure the display settings for your entities.

6.4.2: Panels

Panels is another powerful module that allows you to create custom page layouts and content displays using a drag-and-drop interface. Panels can be used in conjunction with Views, blocks, and other components to create complex and dynamic content displays. Some key features of Panels include:

1. Panel pages: Create custom panel pages with unique URL paths, which can be used to display content, Views, blocks, and other components in a flexible layout.
2. Panel nodes: Create panel nodes that can be used as individual pieces of content within your site, with their own unique layouts and display settings.
3. Panel variants: Define multiple variants of a panel, each with its own layout and display settings, which can be selected based on specific selection criteria or contextual information.

To get started with Panels, install and enable the module, along with its required dependencies, such as the Chaos Tool Suite (ctools) module. Once enabled, you can create custom panel pages, nodes, and variants by navigating to the 'Panels' configuration page under 'Structure' in the admin toolbar.

In conclusion, Display Suite and Panels are powerful tools for creating custom layouts and content displays in Drupal 10 without writing any code. By mastering these modules, you can design visually engaging, contextually relevant, and highly functional content displays that cater to the unique needs of your audience and provide an exceptional user experience.

6.4.2.1: A Deeper Dive into Panels in Drupal 10

Panels in Drupal 10 is a versatile module that allows you to create complex layouts and content displays through a user-friendly, drag-and-drop interface. In this section, we will explore in-depth how to use Panels in Drupal 10 to create custom panel pages, nodes, and variants, as well as integrate Panels with other components such as Views and blocks.

Getting Started with Panels

Before diving into Panels, ensure that the module and its dependencies are installed and enabled. The required dependencies include:

1. Chaos Tool Suite (ctools)
2. Page Manager
3. Panels
4. Panels IPE (In-Place Editor)

Once these modules are installed and enabled, you can begin creating custom panel pages, nodes, and variants.

Creating Panel Pages

Panel pages are standalone pages with custom layouts that can contain various content elements, such as nodes, Views, blocks, and other components. To create a panel page, follow these steps:

1. Navigate to the 'Pages' configuration page under 'Structure' in the admin toolbar.
2. Click the 'Add custom page' button.
3. Enter a title, description, and URL path for your panel page.
4. Configure the settings for the panel page, such as the access settings and menu item.
5. Click the 'Save and continue' button to create the panel page and open the Panels UI for further configuration.

Configuring Panel Page Layouts

Once you have created a panel page, you can configure its layout and content using the Panels UI:

1. Choose a layout for your panel page from the available options or create your own custom layout using the Layout Builder.
2. Add content to your panel page by dragging and dropping components, such as nodes, Views, blocks, and other elements, into the layout's regions.

3. Configure the display settings for each content element, such as the view mode, visibility settings, and contextual filters.
4. Save the panel page and preview it on your site.

Creating Panel Nodes

Panel nodes are individual pieces of content that have their own unique layouts and display settings. To create a panel node, follow these steps:

1. Enable the 'Panelizer' module, which is included with the Panels module.
2. Navigate to the content type configuration page for the content type you want to panelize.
3. Enable panelization for the content type and configure the panelizer settings, such as the default layout and allowed content elements.
4. Create a new node of the panelized content type and configure its layout and content using the Panels UI, similar to configuring a panel page.

Creating Panel Variants

Panel variants are alternative versions of a panel page or node with different layouts and content, which can be selected based on specific criteria or contextual information. To create a panel variant, follow these steps:

1. Navigate to the Panels UI for the panel page or node you want to create a variant for.

2. Click the 'Add variant' button and enter a name and description for the variant.
3. Configure the selection criteria for the variant, such as the user role, URL argument, or other contextual factors.
4. Configure the layout and content for the variant using the Panels UI, similar to configuring a panel page or node.
5. Save the panel page or node and test the variant selection on your site.

Integrating Panels with Views and Blocks

Panels can be integrated with Views and blocks to create powerful and dynamic content displays:

1. Add a View to a panel by selecting the 'View panes' content element in the Panels UI, and then choose the desired View and display type.
2. Add a block to a panel by selecting the 'Block' content

6.4.3: Panelizer vs Layout Builder in Drupal 10

Introduction

In Drupal 10, both Panelizer and Layout Builder offer powerful solutions for creating custom layouts and content displays. While both modules provide similar functionality, they have distinct differences and use cases. In this section, we will compare Panelizer and Layout Builder, highlighting their key features and exploring when to use each module.

Panelizer

Panelizer is a module that extends the functionality of Panels, allowing you to create custom layouts and content displays for individual nodes or other entities. Some key features of Panelizer include:

1. Custom layouts per entity: Panelizer enables you to create unique layouts for each entity, such as nodes, users, or comments.
2. Integration with Panels: Panelizer leverages the Panels module to provide a familiar and powerful drag-and-drop interface for configuring layouts and content.
3. Reusable layouts: Panelizer allows you to define reusable layouts that can be applied to multiple entities of the same type, streamlining the process of creating consistent designs across your site.

Layout Builder

Layout Builder is a core module in Drupal 10 that provides a flexible and user-friendly interface for creating custom layouts and content displays without the need for additional modules or dependencies. Some key features of Layout Builder include:

1. Inline editing: Layout Builder offers a true WYSIWYG experience, allowing you to edit content and configure layouts directly on the page.
2. Layout templates: Layout Builder enables you to create layout templates that can be applied to multiple entities or entity types, simplifying the process of maintaining consistent designs across your site.
3. Block integration: Layout Builder provides seamless integration with Drupal's block system, allowing you to place and configure blocks within your custom layouts.

Comparison and Use Cases

While both Panelizer and Layout Builder offer powerful layout customization tools, there are several key differences between the two modules that may influence which one is best suited for your project:

1. Complexity and dependencies: Panelizer relies on the Panels and Chaos Tool Suite (ctools) modules, making it a more complex solution with additional dependencies. In contrast, Layout Builder is a core module that requires no additional modules or dependencies.
2. Learning curve: Panelizer may have a steeper learning curve due to its integration with Panels and additional configuration options. Layout Builder, on the other hand, offers a more streamlined and intuitive user experience.
3. Flexibility: Panelizer provides more granular control over layouts and content displays, making it a suitable choice for projects with complex design requirements. Layout

Builder offers a simpler and more streamlined approach, making it ideal for projects with more straightforward layout needs.

In conclusion, the choice between Panelizer and Layout Builder in Drupal 10 depends on your project's specific requirements and goals. If you need a more powerful and flexible solution with granular control over layouts and content displays, Panelizer may be the right choice. If you prefer a simpler, more streamlined solution with fewer dependencies and a more intuitive user experience, Layout Builder may be the better option.

Chapter 7: Search and SEO

Search and Search Engine Optimization (SEO) are essential aspects of any successful website, ensuring that users can easily find and access relevant content on your site, and that search engines can effectively index and rank your site in search results. In this extended version of Chapter 7, we will provide an overview of various aspects of search and SEO in Drupal 10, touching upon topics such as site search, metadata, URL structure, and performance optimization. Detailed subchapters will further explore each of these topics, providing guidance on best practices and recommended modules for implementing effective search and SEO strategies in Drupal 10.

7.1: Site Search

An efficient site search is essential for providing users with a seamless experience while navigating your Drupal 10 site. While Drupal comes with built-in search functionality, it can be extended and customized using contributed modules or third-party services to create advanced search capabilities tailored to your site's specific needs.

Built-in Search Functionality

Drupal's core search module provides basic search functionality for content and users, allowing you to create simple search pages and indexes. Although the built-in search is suitable for smaller sites, it may not be the best choice for larger or more complex websites, as it may lack flexibility and performance.

Contributed Modules

Several contributed modules can help enhance Drupal's search capabilities, such as:

1. Search API: This module provides a powerful and flexible framework for creating search indexes and pages, integrating with various backends like the Database Search module and Solr Search module.
2. Database Search: A submodule of Search API, Database Search leverages your site's existing database for search indexing and querying, making it a suitable choice for small to medium-sized websites.
3. Solr Search: Another submodule of Search API, Solr Search integrates with the Apache Solr search platform, offering a high-performance and scalable search solution for large or complex websites.

These modules enable you to build robust search indexes, custom search pages, and search result displays that are fine-tuned to your site's content and requirements.

Third-Party Services

In addition to contributed modules, you can also integrate third-party search services, like Algolia Search, to enhance your site's search capabilities. Algolia is a popular, hosted search solution that provides fast and relevant search results, as well as additional features like typo-tolerance, faceted search, and real-time indexing.

To integrate Algolia with Drupal 10, you can use the Search API Algolia module, which extends the Search API module to support Algolia as a search backend. With this module, you can easily index your Drupal content with Algolia and create custom search pages and displays using the familiar Search API interface.

Steps to integrate Algolia Search with Drupal 10:

1. Sign up for an Algolia account and create an application within their dashboard.
2. Install and enable the Search API Algolia module on your Drupal site.
3. Configure the Search API Algolia module with your Algolia application credentials (Application ID, API Key).
4. Create a new search index using the Search API module and select Algolia as the backend.
5. Configure the index settings, such as the content types to index and the fields to include.
6. Create a search page or view using the Search API module, and configure the display settings as desired.
7. Re-index your content with Algolia and test the search functionality on your site.

In conclusion, Drupal 10 offers a variety of options for implementing powerful site search capabilities, from built-in functionality and contributed modules to third-party services like Algolia Search. By carefully selecting and configuring the right search solution for your specific needs, you can provide your users with a fast, relevant, and user-friendly search experience.

7.2: Metadata

Metadata plays a crucial role in effective SEO by providing valuable information about your site's content and structure to search engines. Implementing proper metadata, such as title tags, meta descriptions, and structured data, can significantly improve your site's search engine ranking and visibility. In this deep dive, we will explore various types of metadata, best practices for metadata implementation, and how to manage metadata in Drupal 10 using the Metatag module.

Types of Metadata

1. Title Tags: The title tag is an HTML element that specifies the title of a webpage. It is displayed as the clickable headline in search engine results and is crucial for both SEO and user experience. A well-crafted title tag should be unique, descriptive, and concise, accurately reflecting the content of the page.
2. Meta Descriptions: The meta description is an HTML attribute that provides a brief summary of a webpage's content. While not directly affecting search rankings,

meta descriptions can influence click-through rates by enticing users to visit your site. A compelling meta description should be informative, unique, and aligned with the page's content.

3. Structured Data: Structured data is a standardized format for providing information about a page and its content to search engines. By using structured data, you can help search engines better understand your content and display it more prominently in search results, such as rich snippets or knowledge panels. Popular structured data formats include JSON-LD, Microdata, and RDFa.

Best Practices for Metadata Implementation

1. Be unique and descriptive: Ensure that your title tags and meta descriptions accurately represent the content of each page and are unique across your site.
2. Optimize for keywords: Incorporate relevant keywords in your title tags and meta descriptions to improve search engine visibility, but avoid keyword stuffing.
3. Follow character limits: Keep title tags under 60 characters and meta descriptions under 160 characters to ensure proper display in search engine results.
4. Use structured data: Implement structured data to provide search engines with additional context about your content and enhance your search result listings.

Managing Metadata in Drupal 10 with the Metatag Module

The Metatag module is a popular choice for managing metadata in Drupal 10, offering a flexible and user-friendly interface for configuring metadata across various content types and pages. With the Metatag module, you can:

1. Define metadata templates: Create reusable metadata templates for various content types, such as articles, events, or products, to ensure consistent metadata implementation across your site.
2. Configure default metadata values: Set default values for title tags, meta descriptions, and structured data to be used when specific metadata is not provided for a page.
3. Override metadata on a per-page basis: Customize metadata for individual pages as needed, allowing for more granular control over your site's metadata.

Steps to manage metadata with the Metatag module:

1. Install and enable the Metatag module on your Drupal 10 site.
2. Navigate to Configuration > Search and metadata > Metatag to access the Metatag settings page.
3. Configure default metadata values for your site, such as the global title tag and meta description.
4. Add metadata templates for various content types by clicking "Add default meta tag."
5. Customize the metadata fields for each template, such as title tags, meta descriptions, and structured data.

6. Override metadata for individual pages or nodes by editing the "Metatags" tab in the content editing interface.

In conclusion, implementing proper metadata is essential for effective SEO in Drupal 10. By following best practices for metadata implementation and leveraging the Metatag module to manage metadata across your site, you can significantly improve your site's search engine ranking and visibility.

7.3: URL Structure

A well-organized and descriptive URL structure is crucial for both user experience and SEO, as it makes it easier for users and search engines to understand and navigate your site's content. In this deep dive, we will explore the importance of a clean URL structure, best practices for creating user-friendly and search engine-friendly URLs, and how to manage URL aliases and patterns in Drupal 10 using the Pathauto and Redirect modules.

Importance of Clean URL Structure

A clean URL structure provides several benefits, including:

1. Improved user experience: Users can easily understand the hierarchy and content of your site by looking at the URLs.

2. Enhanced search engine indexing: Search engines can better interpret and index your site's content based on the URL structure.
3. Better search engine ranking: Descriptive and keyword-rich URLs can help improve your site's search engine ranking.

Best Practices for URL Structure

1. Use descriptive and meaningful URLs: Create URLs that accurately represent the content of the page and include relevant keywords.
2. Keep URLs short and concise: Shorter URLs are easier to read, share, and remember, making them more user-friendly and SEO-friendly.
3. Use hyphens to separate words: Hyphens are the preferred method for separating words in URLs, as they are easier to read and more accessible for screen readers.
4. Avoid dynamic URLs with query parameters: Static, human-readable URLs are easier to understand and index for both users and search engines.
5. Maintain a consistent URL structure: Stick to a consistent URL pattern across your site to make it easier for users to navigate and for search engines to understand your site's hierarchy.

Managing URL Structure in Drupal 10 with Pathauto and Redirect

Drupal 10 provides a flexible system for managing URL aliases and patterns, which can be further extended using modules like Pathauto and Redirect. These modules enable you to create custom URL patterns based on tokens, automate URL alias generation, and manage redirects to ensure a consistent and user-friendly URL structure.

Pathauto

Pathauto is a popular Drupal module that automatically generates URL aliases based on configurable patterns. With Pathauto, you can create custom URL patterns for different content types, taxonomies, and users, using tokens to dynamically build URLs from your site's content.

Steps to configure Pathauto:

1. Install and enable the Pathauto module on your Drupal 10 site.
2. Navigate to Configuration > Search and metadata > URL aliases > Patterns to access the Pathauto settings page.
3. Configure URL patterns for various content types, taxonomy terms, and users by creating new patterns and selecting the appropriate tokens.

Redirect

The Redirect module allows you to manage URL redirects within your Drupal site, ensuring that users and search engines can always find your content, even if its URL changes. With Redirect, you can create manual redirects, automatically generate redirects when a URL alias is updated, and track 404 errors to identify broken links on your site.

Steps to configure Redirect:

1. Install and enable the Redirect module on your Drupal 10 site.
2. Navigate to Configuration > Search and metadata > URL redirects to access the Redirect settings page.
3. Create manual redirects by clicking "Add redirect" and specifying the source and destination paths.
4. Configure automatic redirects by navigating to Configuration > Search and metadata > URL aliases > Settings and enabling the "Automatically create redirects when URL aliases are changed" option.
5. Monitor 404 errors by navigating to Reports > Top 'page not found' errors and creating redirects for frequently encountered broken links.

7.4: XML Sitemaps

XML sitemaps are essential for helping search engines discover and index your site's content. By creating an XML sitemap and submitting it to search engines like Google and Bing, you can ensure that your site's content is accurately and efficiently indexed. The Simple XML Sitemap module is a popular solution for generating XML sitemaps in Drupal 10, offering a range of configuration options and customization features to suit the specific needs of your site.

7.5: Performance Optimization

Optimizing your Drupal 10 site's performance not only improves the user experience but also positively impacts your search engine ranking, as search engines like Google consider page load times when determining rankings. In this deep dive, we will explore various performance optimization techniques for Drupal 10, including caching, image optimization, and code optimization, as well as how to use contributed modules to enhance your site's performance.

Caching

Caching is a crucial performance optimization technique that involves storing and reusing previously generated content, reducing the load on your server and speeding up page load times. Drupal 10 offers a variety of caching options, including:

1. Page Caching: Drupal caches entire rendered pages for anonymous users, significantly reducing server load and response time.
2. Block Caching: Drupal can cache individual blocks on your site, allowing for more granular caching control.
3. Dynamic Page Cache: This module caches portions of a page for both anonymous and authenticated users,

speeding up page load times without compromising personalized content.

To configure caching in Drupal 10:

1. Navigate to Configuration > Performance.
2. Configure the page cache maximum age, which determines how long cached pages are stored before being regenerated.
3. Enable or disable dynamic page cache and block caching as needed.

Image Optimization

Optimizing images can significantly reduce your site's overall size and improve load times. Drupal 10 provides the following options for image optimization:

1. Image Styles: Use Drupal's built-in image styles to automatically resize, crop, and compress images when they are displayed on your site.
2. Lazy Loading: Implement lazy loading to defer the loading of off-screen images until they are needed, reducing the initial page load time.
3. Responsive Images: Use the Responsive Images module to serve appropriately sized images based on the user's device and screen size.

Code Optimization

Optimizing your site's code can help improve performance by reducing the size and complexity of your HTML, CSS, and JavaScript files. Some code optimization techniques include:

1. Minification: Remove unnecessary whitespace, comments, and characters from your code to reduce file size and improve load times.
2. Aggregation: Combine multiple CSS or JavaScript files into a single file to reduce the number of HTTP requests needed to load your site.
3. Defer or async loading of JavaScript: Load JavaScript files asynchronously or after the HTML content has loaded to prevent render-blocking and speed up page load times.

Drupal 10 provides built-in CSS and JavaScript aggregation, which can be enabled by navigating to Configuration > Performance.

Contributed Modules for Performance Optimization

Several contributed modules can further enhance your Drupal 10 site's performance, including:

1. Advanced CSS/JS Aggregation: This module extends Drupal's built-in aggregation features, providing additional options for minification, compression, and bundling of CSS and JavaScript files.

2. Boost: The Boost module creates static HTML pages for your Drupal site, allowing for faster page load times and reduced server load, particularly for anonymous users.
3. Redis or Memcache: These modules integrate with caching backends like Redis or Memcached to provide high-performance, scalable caching solutions.

In conclusion, optimizing your Drupal 10 site's performance is essential for providing a fast, responsive user experience and improving your search engine ranking. By implementing caching, optimizing images and code, and leveraging contributed modules, you can significantly enhance your site's performance and ensure that it loads quickly and efficiently for all users.

7.6: Analytics and Reporting

Monitoring and analyzing your Drupal 10 site's traffic, user behavior, and performance is essential for making data-driven decisions, optimizing user experience, and improving search engine rankings. In this deep dive, we will explore various analytics and reporting tools, including Google Analytics, Google Search Console, and Drupal's built-in reports, as well as best practices for tracking user interactions and conversions.

Google Analytics

Google Analytics is a widely-used web analytics service that allows you to monitor your site's traffic, user behavior, and performance. By integrating Google Analytics with your Drupal

10 site, you can gain valuable insights into how users find and interact with your content, helping you optimize your site's structure, content, and marketing efforts.

To integrate Google Analytics with your Drupal 10 site:

1. Install and enable the Google Analytics module on your Drupal site.
2. Create a Google Analytics account and obtain your tracking ID.
3. Navigate to Configuration > Google Analytics in your Drupal admin interface and enter your tracking ID.
4. Configure any additional tracking settings, such as tracking page views, events, or custom dimensions.

Google Search Console

Google Search Console is a powerful tool for monitoring your site's search performance, identifying crawl errors, and submitting sitemaps. By integrating Google Search Console with your Drupal 10 site, you can ensure that your site is properly indexed by Google and quickly identify and resolve any search-related issues.

To integrate Google Search Console with your Drupal 10 site:

1. Create a Google Search Console account and add your Drupal site as a property.

2. Verify your site ownership using one of the available verification methods, such as adding a meta tag to your site's HTML or uploading an HTML file.
3. Submit your site's XML sitemap to Google Search Console to ensure that your content is crawled and indexed correctly.

Drupal Built-in Reports

Drupal 10 provides several built-in reports that allow you to monitor your site's performance, user activity, and content updates. Some useful Drupal reports include:

1. Top 'page not found' errors: Identify broken links and missing pages on your site.
2. Top search phrases: Understand the search queries users are using within your site.
3. Content updates: Monitor recent content changes and updates made by your site's users.

To access these reports, navigate to Reports in your Drupal admin interface.

Tracking User Interactions and Conversions

Tracking user interactions and conversions on your Drupal 10 site can help you understand how users engage with your content and identify opportunities for optimization. Some common user interactions and conversions that can be tracked include:

1. Form submissions: Monitor the number of users who complete and submit your site's contact, registration, or subscription forms.
2. Button clicks: Track user interactions with call-to-action buttons, such as "Add to Cart" or "Download Now."
3. Video plays: Measure user engagement with embedded video content on your site.

These interactions can be tracked using Google Analytics events or custom dimensions, providing valuable insights into user behavior and the effectiveness of your site's content and design.

In conclusion, analytics and reporting are essential components of effective SEO and site optimization. By leveraging tools like Google Analytics and Google Search Console, as well as Drupal's built-in reports, you can gain valuable insights into your site's performance, user behavior, and search engine visibility. These insights can help you make data-driven decisions to improve your site's structure, content, and marketing efforts, ultimately leading to better search engine rankings and user engagement.

Chapter 8:
Performance and
Security

In this chapter, we will explore the critical aspects of performance and security for your Drupal 10 website. Ensuring your site runs efficiently and is secure from potential threats is essential for providing a great user experience and maintaining your site's reputation. We will cover various topics, including caching, performance optimization, security best practices, and maintaining a secure and up-to-date Drupal installation.

8.1: Caching Strategies

Caching is a fundamental technique for improving the performance of your Drupal 10 site. By temporarily storing and reusing previously generated content, caching reduces the load on your server and speeds up page load times. In this deep dive, we will explore various caching strategies available in Drupal 10, including page caching, block caching, and dynamic page caching, and how to configure and use these strategies to optimize your site's performance.

Page Caching

Page caching involves storing the entire rendered output of a page and serving it to users without regenerating the content. Page caching is particularly effective for anonymous users, as their requests can be served directly from the cache without the need for any server-side processing. To enable page caching in Drupal 10, follow these steps:

1. Navigate to Configuration > Performance.
2. Set the "Page cache maximum age" to a value greater than 0. This determines how long cached pages are stored before being regenerated.

Block Caching

Block caching allows you to cache individual blocks on your site, providing more granular control over caching. This is useful when you have content that is updated more frequently than the rest of the page or when you need to cache specific sections of your site for authenticated users. To enable block caching in Drupal 10, follow these steps:

1. Navigate to Configuration > Performance.
2. Enable "Cache blocks" under the "Block cache" section.

Dynamic Page Cache

Dynamic page caching is a more sophisticated caching strategy that caches portions of a page for both anonymous and authenticated users. This allows you to cache static content while still serving personalized content to authenticated users.

The Dynamic Page Cache module is included with Drupal 10 and can be enabled by following these steps:

1. Navigate to Extend and enable the "Dynamic Page Cache" module.
2. Navigate to Configuration > Performance and ensure that "Cache pages for anonymous users" and "Cache blocks" are enabled.

Configuring Caching Strategies

To fine-tune your caching strategy, you can adjust the cache settings for individual views, blocks, and content types. This allows you to set specific cache lifetimes and cache tags for different sections of your site, providing more control over how and when content is cached.

1. Views: To configure caching settings for a view, navigate to the view's edit page, click on the "Advanced" section, and find the "Caching" settings. From here, you can set the cache lifetime and cache tags for the view.
2. Blocks: To configure caching settings for a block, navigate to the block's edit page and find the "Cache settings" section. From here, you can set the cache lifetime and cache tags for the block.
3. Content Types: To configure caching settings for a content type, navigate to the content type's edit page, click on the "Manage fields" tab, and find the "Cache settings" section. From here, you can set the cache lifetime and cache tags for the content type.

Conclusion

Caching is a crucial aspect of optimizing your Drupal 10 site's performance. By implementing and configuring various caching strategies, such as page caching, block caching, and dynamic page caching, you can significantly reduce server load and improve your site's response time. Understanding and utilizing these caching strategies will ensure that your site remains fast and responsive, providing an excellent user experience for all visitors.

8.2: Performance Optimization

Optimizing the performance of your Drupal 10 site is essential for providing a great user experience and improving search engine rankings. In this deep dive, we will explore various performance optimization techniques, including code optimization, image optimization, and using contributed modules to improve your site's performance. Additionally, we will discuss how to measure and analyze your site's performance using built-in Drupal reports and third-party tools.

Code Optimization

Optimizing your site's code can significantly improve its performance. Some code optimization techniques include:

1. Minify CSS and JavaScript: Minifying CSS and JavaScript files can reduce their size and decrease page load times.

The Advanced CSS/JS Aggregation module can help automate this process.

2. Optimize database queries: Ensure that your custom code and contributed modules use efficient database queries to minimize server load.

3. Use lazy loading: Lazy loading allows you to defer the loading of off-screen content until it is needed, speeding up the initial page load time.

Image Optimization

Optimizing images on your site can have a significant impact on page load times. Some image optimization techniques include:

1. Compress images: Use image compression tools to reduce the file size of your images without sacrificing quality. The ImageAPI Optimize module can help automate this process.

2. Use responsive images: Configure your site to serve different image sizes based on the user's screen size, ensuring that users only download the images they need.

3. Use the picture element: The picture element allows you to serve different image formats (such as WebP) to browsers that support them, further reducing image file sizes.

Contributed Modules

Several contributed modules can help improve your site's performance:

1. Advanced CSS/JS Aggregation (AdvAgg): This module minifies and compresses CSS and JavaScript files, reducing their size and improving page load times.
2. Boost: The Boost module provides static page caching for anonymous users, significantly reducing server load and improving performance.
3. Redis or Memcached: Integrating your site with Redis or Memcached can improve performance by offloading cache storage to a high-performance in-memory data store.

Measuring and Analyzing Performance

To measure and analyze your site's performance, you can use the following tools:

1. Built-in Drupal reports: Drupal 10 provides several built-in reports, such as the Status report and the Top 'page not found' errors report, which can help you identify performance issues and areas for improvement.
2. Web Developer Tools: Browser-based developer tools, such as Google Chrome's DevTools or Firefox's Developer Tools, can help you identify performance bottlenecks, optimize images, and analyze CSS and JavaScript files.
3. Third-party tools: Tools like Google PageSpeed Insights, GTmetrix, and WebPageTest can provide valuable insights into your site's performance and offer suggestions for optimization.

Conclusion

Optimizing the performance of your Drupal 10 site is a critical aspect of providing a great user experience and improving search engine rankings. By implementing various performance optimization techniques, such as code optimization, image optimization, and using contributed modules, you can significantly improve your site's performance. Measuring and analyzing your site's performance using built-in Drupal reports and third-party tools will ensure that your site remains fast, responsive, and provides an excellent user experience for all visitors.

8.3: Security Best Practices

Explore best practices for maintaining a secure Drupal site, including keeping your Drupal core and contributed modules up-to-date, implementing strong user authentication and access control, and following secure coding practices. Understand how to use Drupal's built-in security features, such as input filtering and role-based access control, to protect your site from common security vulnerabilities.

8.4: Regularly Updating Drupal Core and Modules

Learn the importance of keeping your Drupal core and contributed modules up-to-date to ensure the security and stability of your site. Understand the update process and how to use the Update Manager module to check for and apply updates to your site.

8.5: Backup and Recovery Strategies

Discover best practices for backing up your Drupal site, including regular database backups, file system backups, and off-site storage. Learn about various backup tools and modules available for Drupal, such as the Backup and Migrate module, and how to create a disaster recovery plan to ensure your site can quickly recover from data loss or server failures.

8.6: Securing User Authentication and Access Control

Explore techniques for securing user authentication and access control in Drupal, such as implementing two-factor authentication, using strong passwords, and limiting user permissions based on roles. Learn how to monitor user activity and protect your site from brute-force attacks using contributed modules like Security Kit and Flood Control.

8.7: Monitoring and Auditing Your Site's Security

Understand the importance of monitoring and auditing your site's security to identify and address potential vulnerabilities. Learn how to use built-in Drupal reports, such as the Status report and Recent log messages, as well as contributed modules like Security Review, to analyze your site's security configuration and identify areas for improvement.

In conclusion, maintaining optimal performance and security for your Drupal 10 site is crucial for providing a positive user experience and ensuring the safety of your site's data and users. By following best practices for caching, performance optimization, and security, you can ensure that your site remains fast, stable, and secure, allowing you to focus on creating engaging content and providing a great user experience.

Chapter 9: Multilingual and Internationalization

Creating a multilingual and internationalized website is essential for reaching a global audience and providing a great user experience for users from different linguistic and cultural backgrounds. In this chapter, we will explore various features and techniques available in Drupal 10 for building multilingual and internationalized websites, including language detection, content translation, interface translation, and configuration translation.

Conclusion
Building a multilingual and internationalized Drupal 10 site allows you to reach a broader audience and provide a better user experience for users from different linguistic and cultural backgrounds. By leveraging Drupal's built-in features and contributed modules, you can create a site that is easily translated and optimized for a global audience. Understanding and implementing the techniques discussed in this chapter will ensure that your site remains accessible, engaging, and user-friendly for all visitors, regardless of their language or location.

9.1: Language Configuration

Configuring languages for your Drupal 10 site is the first step in creating a multilingual and internationalized website. Drupal 10 makes it easy to add, remove, and manage languages, as well as configure language detection and selection settings. In this extended section, we will provide a detailed guide on configuring languages in Drupal 10 using the built-in Language module.

Adding Languages

To add a new language to your Drupal 10 site, follow these steps:

1. Navigate to Configuration > Regional and language > Languages.
2. Click on the "Add language" button.
3. Select the desired language from the "Language name" dropdown list.
4. Optionally, you can customize the "Language code" and "Language direction" if needed.
5. Click the "Add language" button to add the new language to your site.

Drupal 10 includes translations for many languages, and when you add a new language, Drupal will automatically download the latest translation files for the selected language.

Setting the Default Language

To set the default language for your site, follow these steps:

1. Navigate to Configuration > Regional and language > Languages.
2. Find the language you want to set as the default and click the "Set as default" button in the "Operations" column.

The default language is used as a fallback when no other language is available or when the user's preferred language cannot be determined.

Configuring Language Detection and Selection

To configure language detection and selection settings, follow these steps:

1. Navigate to Configuration > Regional and language > Languages.
2. Click on the "Detection and selection" tab.
3. Enable or disable the desired language detection methods by checking or unchecking the corresponding checkboxes.

Drupal 10 supports several language detection methods, including:

- URL: Detects the user's preferred language based on the URL (e.g., using a language prefix or domain).

- Session: Detects the user's preferred language based on their session data.
- Browser: Detects the user's preferred language based on their browser settings.
- User: Allows users to set their preferred language in their user profile.

After enabling the desired language detection methods, you can adjust their priority by dragging and dropping them in the list. The order in which they appear in the list determines the order in which they are used to detect the user's preferred language.

Customizing Language Settings

If you need to customize language settings, such as language code, language direction, or language name, follow these steps:

1. Navigate to Configuration > Regional and language > Languages.
2. Find the language you want to edit and click the "Edit" button in the "Operations" column.
3. Modify the desired settings and click the "Save language" button to save your changes.

Conclusion

Language configuration is the foundation of building a multilingual and internationalized Drupal 10 site. By adding languages, setting the default language, and configuring language detection and selection settings, you can create a website that caters to a diverse audience with varying linguistic and cultural backgrounds. Understanding and properly configuring language settings in Drupal 10 will ensure that your site remains accessible, engaging, and user-friendly for all visitors, regardless of their language or location.

9.2: Content Translation

Content translation is a crucial aspect of creating a multilingual and internationalized website in Drupal 10. By translating your site's content, you ensure that users from different linguistic backgrounds can access and engage with your site. In this deep dive, we will explore how to use the Content Translation module to enable content translation, manage translated content, and streamline the translation process using the Translation Management Tool (TMGMT) module.

Enabling Content Translation

To enable content translation for your Drupal 10 site, follow these steps:

1. Ensure the Content Translation module is installed and enabled. If not, go to Extend and enable the module.
2. Navigate to Configuration > Regional and language > Content language and translation.

3. Check the "Enable translation" checkbox for the content types you want to translate.
4. Click the "Save configuration" button to save your changes.

Now you can create and manage translations for the selected content types.

Creating and Managing Translated Content

To create a translation for a piece of content, follow these steps:

1. Navigate to the content you want to translate (e.g., a node, block, or taxonomy term).
2. Click the "Translate" tab.
3. Click the "Add" button next to the language you want to translate the content into.
4. Fill out the translation form with the translated content.
5. Click the "Save" button to save the translation.

The translated content is now available on your site, and Drupal will automatically display the appropriate translation based on the user's preferred language.

To manage and edit translations, follow these steps:

1. Navigate to the content you want to manage (e.g., a node, block, or taxonomy term).
2. Click the "Translate" tab.

3. You can now view all the available translations for the content.
4. To edit a translation, click the "Edit" button next to the desired language.
5. Make the necessary changes and click the "Save" button to save your updates.

Using the Translation Management Tool (TMGMT) Module

The Translation Management Tool (TMGMT) module helps streamline the content translation process by providing a centralized dashboard to manage translations, integrating with external translation services, and supporting translation workflows.

To use the TMGMT module, follow these steps:

1. Download and install the TMGMT module from Drupal.org or using Composer.
2. Enable the TMGMT module and any additional submodules required for your specific use case (e.g., TMGMT Translator, TMGMT Content, or TMGMT UI).
3. Configure the TMGMT module by navigating to Configuration > Regional and language > Translation management settings.
4. Set up your desired translation workflow, assign translation roles, and configure any external translation services, if needed.

Once the TMGMT module is configured, you can manage translations by navigating to Content > Translation Management. From here, you can create translation jobs, assign translations to users or external services, and track translation progress.

Conclusion

Content translation is essential for creating a multilingual and internationalized Drupal 10 site. By enabling content translation, creating and managing translated content, and leveraging the power of the TMGMT module, you can provide a seamless user experience for visitors from different linguistic backgrounds. Implementing content translation effectively will ensure your site remains accessible, engaging, and user-friendly for all users, regardless of their language or location.

9.3: Interface Translation

Interface translation is a critical component of a multilingual and internationalized website, as it allows users to interact with your site in their preferred language. In this deep dive, we will explore how to use the Interface Translation module in Drupal 10 to translate the user interface (UI), manage translations for custom and contributed modules, and keep translations up-to-date with the Localization Update module.

Enabling Interface Translation

To enable interface translation in Drupal 10, follow these steps:

1. Ensure that the Interface Translation module is installed and enabled. If not, go to Extend and enable the module.
2. After enabling the module, Drupal will automatically import the latest translation files for the languages you have configured on your site.

Translating the User Interface

To translate the user interface, follow these steps:

1. Navigate to Configuration > Regional and language > User interface translation.
2. Use the "Filter" options to search for specific strings or limit the search to specific modules or text groups.
3. Click the "Edit" button next to the string you want to translate.
4. Enter the translation for the desired language(s) and click the "Save translations" button to save your changes.

Importing and Exporting Translation Files

To import or export translation files, follow these steps:

1. Navigate to Configuration > Regional and language > User interface translation.
2. Click on the "Import" or "Export" tab, depending on the action you want to perform.

For importing translations:

1. Select the desired language from the dropdown list.
2. Choose a file to upload (in .po format) or paste the contents of the .po file into the "Import translations" text box.
3. Click the "Import" button to import the translations.

For exporting translations:

1. Select the desired language and components (modules, themes, or text groups) from the dropdown lists.
2. Click the "Export" button to download a .po file containing the translations.

Managing Translations for Custom and Contributed Modules

If you create custom modules or use contributed modules that do not have translations available for your site's languages, you can create and manage translations for these modules using the Interface Translation module:

1. Navigate to Configuration > Regional and language > User interface translation.
2. Use the "Filter" options to search for specific strings or limit the search to specific modules.
3. Click the "Edit" button next to the string you want to translate.

4. Enter the translation for the desired language(s) and click the "Save translations" button to save your changes.

Keeping Translations Up-to-Date with the Localization Update Module

The Localization Update module helps keep translations up-to-date by automatically downloading and updating translation files for core, contributed, and custom modules and themes:

1. Download and install the Localization Update module from Drupal.org or using Composer.
2. Enable the Localization Update module in the Extend section.
3. Navigate to Configuration > Regional and language > Localization update settings.
4. Configure the module according to your preferences, such as choosing the update source, setting update intervals, and selecting components to update.
5. Click the "Save configuration" button to save your changes.

After configuring the Localization Update module, it will periodically check for translation updates and apply them to your site.

Conclusion

Interface translation is essential for creating a multilingual and internationalized Drupal 10 site. By translating the user interface, managing translations for custom and contributed modules, and keeping translations up-to-date with the Localization Update module, you can provide a seamless user experience for visitors from different linguistic backgrounds. Implementing interface translation effectively will ensure your site remains accessible, engaging, and user-friendly for all users, regardless of their language or location.

9.4: Configuration Translation

Configuration translation is a critical aspect of building a multilingual and internationalized website in Drupal 10, as it ensures that the site's configuration is available in different languages. Configuration includes elements such as site name, views, blocks, and menus. In this deep dive, we will explore how to use the Configuration Translation module to translate the site's configuration and synchronize translations across different languages.

Enabling Configuration Translation

To enable configuration translation in Drupal 10, follow these steps:

1. Ensure that the Configuration Translation module is installed and enabled. If not, go to Extend and enable the module.
2. After enabling the module, Drupal will automatically import the latest translation files for the languages you have configured on your site.

Translating Configuration Elements

To translate configuration elements, follow these steps:

1. Navigate to the configuration element you want to translate (e.g., a view, block, or menu).
2. Click the "Translate" tab.
3. Click the "Add" button next to the language you want to translate the configuration element into.
4. Fill out the translation form with the translated configuration information.
5. Click the "Save" button to save the translation.

The translated configuration is now available on your site, and Drupal will automatically display the appropriate translation based on the user's preferred language.

Synchronizing Translations Across Languages

In some cases, you may want to synchronize translations across different languages. For example, if you have a multilingual menu with the same structure in all languages, you can use the Configuration Synchronization module to synchronize menu items across languages:

1. Download and install the Configuration Synchronization module from Drupal.org or using Composer.
2. Enable the Configuration Synchronization module in the Extend section.
3. Navigate to Configuration > Development > Configuration synchronization > Translate and synchronize configurations.
4. Select the configuration elements you want to synchronize, such as menus or blocks.
5. Choose the source and target languages for the synchronization.
6. Click the "Synchronize" button to synchronize the translations.

After synchronizing the translations, the configuration elements will be consistent across the selected languages.

Conclusion

Configuration translation is essential for creating a multilingual and internationalized Drupal 10 site. By translating configuration elements and synchronizing translations across languages, you can provide a seamless user experience for visitors from different linguistic backgrounds. Implementing configuration translation effectively will ensure that your site remains accessible, engaging, and user-friendly for all users, regardless of their language or location.

9.5: Translation Workflows and Best Practices

Managing translations effectively is crucial for creating and maintaining a multilingual and internationalized Drupal 10 site. In this deep dive, we will explore various translation workflows and best practices to help streamline the translation process, improve collaboration among team members, and ensure consistent, high-quality translations throughout your site.

Translation Workflows

The translation workflow you choose will depend on your project's requirements and resources. Some common translation workflows include:

1. Manual translations by site administrators: Site administrators create and manage translations directly within the Drupal interface.
2. Collaborative translations by a team: A team of translators collaborates on translations, leveraging Drupal's built-in translation management features and the Translation Management Tool (TMGMT) module to coordinate translation tasks and track progress.
3. Integration with external translation services: Drupal integrates with third-party translation services, such as Lingotek or Gengo, to handle translations. Translators access the Drupal interface or work directly within the external translation service's platform.
4. Machine translations: Use machine translation services, such as Google Translate or DeepL, to automatically generate translations. These translations can be refined manually by human translators as needed.

Best Practices

To improve translation efficiency, maintain consistency, and ensure high-quality translations, consider the following best practices:

1. Plan your translation strategy: Define your translation goals, identify the languages you need to support, and

establish a clear translation workflow. Consider factors such as your target audience, available resources, and budget constraints.

2. Leverage Drupal's built-in translation features: Make full use of Drupal's translation capabilities, such as content, interface, and configuration translation, to provide a consistent and seamless user experience.

3. Use the TMGMT module: The TMGMT module can help streamline the translation process by providing a centralized dashboard for managing translations, integrating with external translation services, and supporting translation workflows.

4. Maintain a translation style guide and glossary: A translation style guide and glossary help ensure consistent terminology and tone across your site. Share these resources with your translation team and update them regularly.

5. Optimize translation workflows with automation: Automate tasks where possible, such as updating translations with the Localization Update module or synchronizing configuration translations with the Configuration Synchronization module.

6. Conduct regular translation audits: Periodically review your site's translations to ensure consistency, accuracy, and adherence to your translation style guide.

7. Collaborate and communicate: Encourage collaboration and open communication among your translation team members. Foster a culture of feedback and continuous improvement.

8. Monitor translation performance: Track translation progress and performance using analytics and reporting tools. Identify areas for improvement and adjust your translation strategy as needed.

Conclusion

Implementing effective translation workflows and best practices is essential for creating and maintaining a multilingual and internationalized Drupal 10 site. By streamlining the translation process, improving collaboration, and ensuring consistent, high-quality translations, you can provide a seamless user experience for visitors from different linguistic backgrounds. Embracing these best practices will help your site remain accessible, engaging, and user-friendly for all users, regardless of their language or location.

9.6: Multilingual SEO

Multilingual SEO is a critical aspect of managing a multilingual and internationalized website, as it ensures that your content is easily discoverable and accessible to users across different languages and regions. In this deep dive, we will explore key strategies and best practices for optimizing your Drupal 10 site for multilingual search engine optimization (SEO).

1. URL Structure and Language Detection

A well-structured URL is essential for multilingual SEO. Use separate URLs for each language version of your site to help search engines index your content accurately. In Drupal 10, you can configure the URL structure for each language using the following steps:

1. Navigate to Configuration > Regional and language > Languages.
2. Click the "Detection and selection" tab.
3. Configure the URL language detection method, such as using a language prefix (e.g., example.com/en/ and example.com/es/) or subdomain (e.g., en.example.com and es.example.com).
4. Save the configuration.
5. Hreflang Tags

Hreflang tags are HTML link elements that help search engines understand the relationship between different language versions of a page. Drupal 10 automatically adds hreflang tags to your site's head section when the Language module is enabled. Ensure that your site has proper hreflang tags for each language version to improve search engine indexing and avoid duplicate content issues.

3. Metadata and Content Translation

Optimize metadata, such as title tags and meta descriptions, for each language version of your site. Translate your metadata to provide users with relevant, engaging information in their preferred language. Use the Metatag module in Drupal to manage and customize metadata for different language versions easily.

4. Sitemaps

Create separate XML sitemaps for each language version of your site to help search engines crawl and index your multilingual content more effectively. Use the XML Sitemap module in Drupal to generate and manage XML sitemaps for each language automatically.

5. Language-Specific Content Promotion

Promote your multilingual content using language-specific keywords and strategies to reach your target audience effectively. Research and identify relevant keywords for each language version of your site, and incorporate these keywords into your content, metadata, and URLs.

6. Localized Link Building

Build high-quality, localized backlinks for each language version of your site to improve its search engine ranking and visibility. Focus on securing backlinks from reputable, language-specific websites and directories to establish your site's authority and relevance in each target market.

7. Analytics and Reporting

Monitor the performance of your multilingual SEO efforts using analytics and reporting tools, such as Google Analytics or Matomo. Track key metrics, such as organic search traffic, bounce rate, and conversion rate, for each language version of your site. Use these insights to refine your multilingual SEO strategy and improve your site's performance.

Conclusion

Effective multilingual SEO is essential for reaching a diverse audience and ensuring that your Drupal 10 site is easily discoverable and accessible to users across different languages and regions. By implementing key strategies and best practices, such as optimizing your URL structure, using hreflang tags, translating metadata and content, and building localized backlinks, you can improve your site's search engine ranking and visibility in each target market. Embrace these best practices to ensure that your multilingual and internationalized site remains accessible, engaging, and user-friendly for all users, regardless of their language or location.

Chapter 10: E-commerce with Drupal

E-commerce has become an essential aspect of modern business, and Drupal offers a variety of tools and modules to help you create a powerful, feature-rich online store. In this deep dive, we will explore the key components of building an e-commerce site with Drupal, including the selection of the right e-commerce platform, the creation of product catalogs, the management of orders and payments, and the optimization of the user experience.

1. Selecting the Right E-commerce Platform

When building an e-commerce site with Drupal, Drupal Commerce is a popular and robust option that provides a wide range of features and integrations to help you create a fully functional online store. Evaluate the platform's features, flexibility, and ease of use to determine if it best suits your needs.

2. Creating Product Catalogs

A well-organized product catalog is essential for a successful e-commerce site. Drupal's flexible content types and taxonomy system make it easy to create and manage product catalogs with custom attributes and categories. Consider using the following modules to enhance your product catalog:

- Commerce Product: Provides a product entity type for creating and managing products in Drupal Commerce.
- Commerce Product Attributes: Allows you to create and manage custom product attributes, such as color or size.
- Facets: Enables the creation of faceted search and navigation for your product catalog, making it easier for customers to find and filter products.
3. Managing Orders and Payments

To manage orders and payments in your Drupal e-commerce site, you'll need to configure various aspects, such as payment gateways, shipping methods, and tax calculations. Drupal Commerce provides robust tools for managing orders and payments, including integration with popular payment gateways like PayPal, Stripe, and Authorize.Net. Additionally, consider using the following modules to enhance your order and payment management capabilities:

- Commerce Shipping: Provides shipping method configuration and calculation tools for Drupal Commerce.
- Commerce Tax: Offers tax calculation and configuration options for Drupal Commerce.

4. Optimizing the User Experience

A seamless and engaging user experience is critical for attracting and retaining customers on your e-commerce site. Drupal offers a variety of modules and tools to help you optimize the user experience, including:

- Commerce Cart: Provides a customizable shopping cart block and management tools for Drupal Commerce.
- Commerce Checkout: Offers a configurable and customizable checkout process for Drupal Commerce.
- Commerce Wishlist: Allows customers to create and manage wishlists in Drupal Commerce.
5. Marketing and Promotions

Effective marketing and promotions are essential for driving sales and increasing customer loyalty. Leverage Drupal's built-in marketing and promotion tools, as well as third-party integrations, to create targeted marketing campaigns, offer discounts and promotions, and track the success of your efforts. Some popular marketing and promotion modules include:

- Commerce Coupons: Enables the creation and management of coupon codes for Drupal Commerce.
- Commerce Discounts: Allows you to create and manage discounts for Drupal Commerce.
- Google Analytics: Integrates Google Analytics with your Drupal site to track user behavior and e-commerce transactions.

Conclusion

Building an e-commerce site with Drupal can be a powerful and flexible solution for your online business. By selecting the right e-commerce platform, creating a well-organized product catalog, managing orders and payments effectively, optimizing the user experience, and implementing effective marketing and promotions, you can create a successful, engaging, and user-friendly e-commerce site that meets the needs of your customers and drives sales. Embrace the full potential of Drupal's e-commerce capabilities to ensure that your online store is a powerful and effective tool for growing your business.

10.1. Drupal Commerce Overview

Drupal Commerce is a comprehensive and flexible e-commerce solution for Drupal websites, designed to provide a seamless integration between content management and online store functionality. In this deep dive, we will explore the key features and capabilities of Drupal Commerce, as well as its modular architecture, which enables you to tailor your e-commerce site to your specific needs.

Key Features and Capabilities

1. Customizable Product Types and Attributes: Drupal Commerce allows you to create custom product types and attributes, enabling you to manage a diverse range of products with different characteristics, such as size, color, or material. This flexibility ensures that your

e-commerce site can accommodate your unique product catalog and display relevant product information to your customers.

2. Dynamic Shopping Cart and Checkout Process: Drupal Commerce provides a dynamic shopping cart and a configurable checkout process that can be customized to match your business requirements. This includes the ability to add, remove, or modify checkout steps, as well as the option to integrate third-party payment gateways and shipping providers.

3. Order Management and Payment Processing: Drupal Commerce offers robust order management and payment processing capabilities, including support for multiple currencies and tax rates, integration with popular payment gateways, and the ability to manage orders, invoices, and shipments through a user-friendly administrative interface.

4. Promotions and Discounts: With Drupal Commerce, you can easily create and manage promotions and discounts for your online store. This includes the ability to create coupon codes, configure percentage-based or fixed-amount discounts, and apply conditions to ensure promotions are only applied to specific products, customers, or order amounts.

5. Multilingual and Multi-Currency Support: Drupal Commerce is designed to support multilingual and multi-currency e-commerce sites, making it an ideal solution for businesses with a global customer base. This includes automatic currency conversion, language-based product catalogs, and translation of

user interface elements, such as buttons and form fields.

Modular Architecture

Drupal Commerce is built on a modular architecture, which allows you to extend and customize its functionality by installing additional modules. This modular approach ensures that your e-commerce site can grow and adapt to meet your evolving business needs. Some popular Drupal Commerce modules include:

1. Commerce Shipping: Provides shipping method configuration and calculation tools for Drupal Commerce, as well as integration with popular shipping providers like UPS, FedEx, and USPS.
2. Commerce Tax: Offers tax calculation and configuration options for Drupal Commerce, including support for VAT, sales tax, and custom tax rates.
3. Commerce Stock: Allows you to manage and track inventory levels for your products, ensuring that you can efficiently fulfill customer orders and maintain accurate stock levels.
4. Commerce Recurring: Enables the creation and management of subscription-based products and services, allowing you to offer recurring billing and automatic renewals to your customers.

Conclusion

Drupal Commerce is a powerful and flexible e-commerce solution for Drupal websites, providing a comprehensive set of features and capabilities that can be customized to meet your unique business requirements. By leveraging its modular architecture and extensive range of available modules, you can create a feature-rich, user-friendly online store that seamlessly integrates with your Drupal site's content management capabilities. Embrace the power and flexibility of Drupal Commerce to build a successful e-commerce site that drives sales, engages customers, and grows your business.

10.2. Setting Up a Product Catalog

Creating an organized and easily navigable product catalog is essential for a successful e-commerce site. In this deep dive, we'll explore how to set up a product catalog using Drupal Commerce, including creating custom product types and attributes, organizing products with taxonomy, and using Views to display your products in a flexible and customizable manner.

1. Custom Product Types and Attributes

Drupal Commerce allows you to create custom product types to accommodate the unique characteristics of your products. Product types are similar to content types in Drupal and can have specific fields and attributes associated with them.

To create a custom product type:

a. Navigate to Commerce > Configuration > Product settings > Product types.

b. Click "Add product type" and enter the required information, such as the name and description of the product type.

c. Save the product type and proceed to add custom fields and attributes as needed.

For example, if you're selling clothing items, you might create a "Clothing" product type with attributes like size, color, and material. These attributes will allow you to define variations of the same product with different characteristics.

2. Organizing Products with Taxonomy

Taxonomy is a powerful tool in Drupal for organizing and categorizing content, and it can also be used to categorize products in your Drupal Commerce store. By creating taxonomies for your product catalog, you can make it easier for customers to find and filter products based on categories or other criteria.

To create a product taxonomy:

a. Navigate to Structure > Taxonomy.

b. Click "Add vocabulary" and enter the required information, such as the name and description of the vocabulary.

c. Save the vocabulary and proceed to add terms representing categories or other classification criteria.

Once you've created a taxonomy vocabulary, you can associate it with your product types by adding a term reference field to the product type's configuration.

    3.   Displaying Products with Views

Views is a powerful tool in Drupal that allows you to create custom displays of content, including products in your Drupal Commerce store. By creating Views for your product catalog, you can create custom product listings, featured product displays, and more.

To create a product view:

a. Navigate to Structure > Views.

b. Click "Add view" and enter the required information, such as the name, description, and display format of the view.

c. In the "Show" dropdown, select "Commerce Product" and configure additional settings as needed.

d. Save the view and proceed to customize it by adding fields, filters, and other configuration options.

For example, you might create a view that displays products in a grid format, with filters for taxonomy terms, price, or other attributes. This can help customers find the products they're looking for and improve their shopping experience.

4. Enhancing Product Catalog Functionality

You can further enhance your product catalog functionality with additional Drupal Commerce modules, such as:

- Commerce Facets: Integrates with the Facets module to provide faceted search and navigation for your product catalog.
- Commerce Search API: Improves the search functionality of your product catalog by integrating with the Search API module, which allows for more flexible and customizable search configurations.

Conclusion

Setting up a well-organized and easily navigable product catalog is crucial for the success of your e-commerce site. Drupal Commerce provides the tools and flexibility to create custom product types and attributes, organize products using taxonomy, and display products with custom Views. By leveraging these features and enhancing your product catalog functionality with additional modules, you can create a user-friendly and efficient shopping experience for your customers, ultimately driving sales and growing your business.

10.3. Managing Orders and Payments

Effectively managing orders and payments is crucial to the success of any e-commerce site. In this deep dive, we'll explore how Drupal Commerce can help you manage orders and payments, including setting up payment gateways, configuring shipping methods, handling tax calculations, and managing customer orders through the administrative interface.

1. Payment Gateways

Payment gateways are essential for processing payments on your e-commerce site. Drupal Commerce supports a wide range of popular payment gateways, including PayPal, Stripe, and Authorize.Net, among others. To set up a payment gateway:

a. Install the appropriate payment gateway module for Drupal Commerce. For example, if you want to use PayPal, install the Commerce PayPal module.

b. Navigate to Commerce > Configuration > Payment gateways.

c. Click "Add payment gateway" and select the payment gateway you want to configure.

d. Enter the required information, such as API credentials, and configure additional settings as needed.

e. Save the payment gateway configuration.

   2.   Shipping Methods

Shipping methods are necessary for calculating shipping costs and providing options to your customers. Drupal Commerce offers various shipping method modules, such as Commerce Shipping, which provides a flexible framework for configuring shipping methods and rates. To set up a shipping method:

a. Install the appropriate shipping method module for Drupal Commerce. For example, if you want to use flat-rate shipping, install the Commerce Flat Rate module.

b. Navigate to Commerce > Configuration > Shipping methods.

c. Click "Add shipping method" and select the shipping method you want to configure.

d. Enter the required information, such as the shipping rate and conditions, and configure additional settings as needed.

e. Save the shipping method configuration.

   3.   Tax Calculations

Handling tax calculations is another essential aspect of managing orders and payments. Drupal Commerce provides a flexible tax calculation system that supports various tax types, such as VAT, sales tax, and custom tax rates. To set up tax calculations:

a. Install the Commerce Tax module, which is part of the core Drupal Commerce package.

b. Navigate to Commerce > Configuration > Taxes.

c. Click "Add tax type" and enter the required information, such as the tax rate and the conditions under which the tax should be applied.

d. Save the tax type configuration.

4. Order Management

Order management involves tracking and processing customer orders, including managing order statuses, invoices, and shipments. Drupal Commerce provides a user-friendly administrative interface for managing orders, allowing you to:

a. View and search for orders based on criteria such as order status, customer, or date.

b. Edit and update order information, including customer details, products, and shipping information.

c. Process order payments, refunds, and cancellations.

d. Manage order statuses, such as marking orders as completed or pending.

5. Enhancing Order and Payment Management

Several additional modules can further enhance your order and payment management capabilities in Drupal Commerce. Some popular options include:

- Commerce Reports: Provides reporting and analytics tools for your e-commerce site, including order summaries, sales data, and customer statistics.
- Commerce Invoice: Generates invoices for customer orders, allowing you to manage and track payments more effectively.
- Commerce Stock: Enables inventory management for your products, ensuring accurate stock levels and efficient order fulfillment.

Conclusion

Effectively managing orders and payments is critical to the success of your e-commerce site. Drupal Commerce provides robust tools for managing orders and payments, including support for popular payment gateways, flexible shipping methods, and comprehensive tax calculations. By leveraging these tools and enhancing your order and payment management capabilities with additional modules, you can create a streamlined and efficient e-commerce experience for both you and your customers.

10.4. Customizing Your Store's Appearance

The appearance of your online store plays a significant role in the customer experience and can ultimately impact sales and customer retention. In this deep dive, we'll explore how to customize your Drupal Commerce store's appearance, including working with themes, creating custom templates, and using layout tools like Display Suite and Layout Builder.

1. Themes

A theme in Drupal defines the visual appearance of your website, including layout, colors, and typography. There are many contributed Drupal themes available that are specifically designed for e-commerce sites, or you can create a custom theme that perfectly matches your brand and requirements.

a. To install a contributed theme, download and enable the theme from the Drupal.org project page, then navigate to Appearance and set the new theme as the default.

b. To create a custom theme, follow Drupal's theme development guidelines, which include creating a .info.yml file, defining theme regions, and creating Twig templates for your theme.

2. Custom Templates

Custom templates are an essential tool for customizing the appearance of your Drupal Commerce store. These templates define how specific elements, such as product pages or shopping carts, are displayed on your site.

a. To create a custom template, locate the default template file for the element you want to customize. For example, for a product page, the default template is "commerce-product.html.twig."

b. Copy the default template file to your theme's "templates" folder and modify it to match your desired design.

c. Clear the cache to apply the changes.

3. Display Suite

Display Suite is a powerful Drupal module that allows you to customize the layout and display of your content, including products, without writing code. With Display Suite, you can create custom view modes, add fields, and rearrange the layout of your product pages.

a. Install the Display Suite module and enable it.

b. Navigate to Structure > Display modes > View modes, and create a new view mode for your product type.

c. Edit the product type's display settings and select the new view mode.

d. Use the drag-and-drop interface to customize the layout and fields for the product display.

4. Layout Builder

Layout Builder is a core Drupal module that provides a visual interface for creating and editing page layouts. It can be used to customize the appearance of your Drupal Commerce store, including product pages, shopping cart pages, and checkout pages.

a. Enable the Layout Builder module.

b. Navigate to the display settings of the element you want to customize, such as the product type or the shopping cart block.

c. Enable the Layout Builder for the element and use the visual interface to add, rearrange, and configure blocks, fields, and sections.

5. Enhancing Your Store's Appearance

Several additional modules and tools can help you further enhance your Drupal Commerce store's appearance:

- Colorbox: Integrates with Drupal Commerce to create a lightbox effect for product images, providing a more engaging and interactive image display.
- Commerce Price Slider: Adds a price range slider to your product catalog, allowing customers to filter products based on price.
- Font Awesome: Integrates the Font Awesome icon library with Drupal, enabling you to easily add scalable vector icons to your store's design.

Conclusion

Customizing your Drupal Commerce store's appearance is essential for providing a unique and engaging shopping experience for your customers. By leveraging themes, custom templates, and layout tools like Display Suite and Layout Builder, you can create a visually appealing and user-friendly e-commerce site that reflects your brand and supports your business goals. Additionally, enhancing your store's appearance with contributed modules and tools can further improve the customer experience, leading to increased sales and customer retention.

Chapter 11:
Integrating with
Third-Party Services

In this chapter, we will discuss the importance of integrating third-party services into your Drupal website and the various benefits they can provide. Third-party services can enhance your site's functionality, improve user experience, and help streamline your business processes. Integrating these services into your Drupal site can be achieved using contributed modules, custom modules, or external libraries.

Some of the key third-party services that can be integrated with Drupal include:

1. Analytics and Tracking: Implementing tracking and analytics tools, such as Google Analytics, can provide valuable insights into your site's performance, visitor behavior, and user engagement.
2. Marketing Automation: Integrating marketing automation platforms, like Mailchimp or HubSpot, can help you manage and optimize your email marketing campaigns, lead generation, and customer nurturing processes.

3. Customer Relationship Management (CRM): Connecting your Drupal site with CRM platforms, such as Salesforce or Zoho CRM, can help streamline customer data management, lead tracking, and sales processes.
4. Payment Processing: Integrating popular payment gateways, like PayPal, Stripe, or Authorize.Net, is essential for processing payments on your e-commerce site securely and efficiently.
5. Social Media Integration: Incorporating social media platforms, such as Facebook, Twitter, or LinkedIn, can help increase your site's visibility, drive traffic, and foster user engagement.
6. Search and Indexing: Implementing third-party search services, like Algolia or Elasticsearch, can improve your site's search functionality, providing faster and more accurate search results.
7. Mapping and Geolocation: Integrating mapping services, such as Google Maps or OpenStreetMap, can enhance your site's geolocation capabilities, allowing users to search for locations, calculate distances, and visualize data on maps.
8. Content Delivery Networks (CDN): Connecting your Drupal site with a CDN, like Cloudflare or Fastly, can improve site performance, decrease load times, and enhance user experience.

In the following subchapters, we will explore each of these third-party services in more detail, discussing their benefits, use cases, and how to integrate them into your Drupal website. We will also provide examples of contributed modules and custom implementation methods that can be used to achieve seamless integration with these services.

11.1. API and Web Services Basics

APIs (Application Programming Interfaces) and web services are the cornerstones of modern web development, enabling seamless communication and data exchange between different applications and services. In this deep dive, we'll explore the basics of APIs and web services, as well as how they relate to Drupal and can be leveraged to integrate third-party services into your Drupal site.

1. APIs

An API is a set of rules, protocols, and tools that allow different software applications to communicate with each other. APIs are used to request and send data between applications, typically over the internet. They enable developers to build applications that can interact with other services and access their features and data.

Some common types of APIs include:

a. REST (Representational State Transfer) APIs: A popular architectural style for designing networked applications, REST APIs use HTTP methods (GET, POST, PUT, DELETE) to perform operations on resources, which are represented as URLs.

b. GraphQL APIs: A query language and runtime for APIs, GraphQL enables clients to request only the data they need, reducing the amount of data transferred and improving performance.

c. SOAP (Simple Object Access Protocol) APIs: A protocol for exchanging structured information in the implementation of web services, SOAP uses XML for its message format and can be transported over various lower-level protocols, including HTTP and SMTP.

2. Web Services

Web services are applications or systems that are accessible over the internet and communicate using standard protocols, such as HTTP or XML. Web services can be used to provide specific functionalities or data to other applications, facilitating integration and interoperability.

There are two primary types of web services:

a. SOAP-based web services: These use the SOAP protocol to exchange information, often relying on WSDL (Web Services Description Language) to describe the service's interface and operations.

b. RESTful web services: These adhere to the principles of REST architecture and use standard HTTP methods to interact with resources.

3. Integrating APIs and Web Services with Drupal

Drupal's flexible architecture makes it an excellent platform for integrating APIs and web services. There are several approaches to achieve this integration, including:

a. Contributed modules: Many contributed modules exist to integrate popular third-party services with Drupal, such as the Google Analytics module, Mailchimp module, or Salesforce Suite. These modules typically provide pre-built API integrations and easy-to-use interfaces for configuring and managing the integration.

b. Custom modules: In some cases, you may need to create a custom module to integrate a specific API or web service with your Drupal site. This can be achieved using Drupal's HTTP client, Guzzle, to make API requests and handle responses. Additionally, Drupal's Plugin API and Services API can be used to create custom plugins and services that interact with external APIs.

c. External libraries: Some third-party services provide SDKs (Software Development Kits) or libraries that can be used to interact with their APIs. These libraries can be included in your custom Drupal modules using Composer, providing a convenient way to work with the API.

Conclusion

APIs and web services are essential tools for modern web development, enabling seamless integration between applications and services. Understanding the basics of APIs and web services, as well as how they can be integrated with Drupal, is critical for building websites that leverage the power of third-party services to enhance functionality, improve user experience, and streamline business processes. By leveraging contributed modules, custom modules, and external libraries, you can harness the power of APIs and web services to create powerful and feature-rich Drupal sites.

11.2. Connecting Drupal with Social Media

Integrating social media platforms into your Drupal site is essential for increasing visibility, driving user engagement, and fostering community interaction. In this deep dive, we'll explore the benefits of connecting Drupal with social media and provide an overview of some common methods and contributed modules for integrating popular social media platforms, such as Facebook, Twitter, Instagram, and LinkedIn.

1. Benefits of Social Media Integration

Some key benefits of integrating social media platforms with your Drupal site include:

a. Increased traffic: Sharing content on social media can drive traffic to your website, potentially resulting in higher conversion rates and increased sales.

b. Enhanced user engagement: Allowing users to interact with your site through social media can foster community interaction and increase user retention.

c. Improved search engine rankings: Social media integration can contribute to your site's SEO, as search engines often consider social signals when ranking websites.

2. Social Media Integration Methods

There are several methods to integrate social media platforms with your Drupal site, including:

a. Social sharing buttons: Add buttons to your site that allow users to share your content on their social media profiles, increasing visibility and potentially driving traffic.

b. Social media feeds: Display your social media content directly on your Drupal site, keeping users engaged and encouraging them to follow your social media profiles.

c. Social login: Allow users to log in or register on your site using their social media accounts, simplifying the registration process and increasing user retention.

3. Contributed Modules for Social Media Integration

Many contributed modules are available for integrating Drupal with popular social media platforms. Some notable examples include:

a. AddToAny Share Buttons: This module enables you to add social sharing buttons for various platforms, such as Facebook, Twitter, LinkedIn, and Pinterest, to your Drupal site. The module is highly customizable, allowing you to choose from various button styles and placement options.

b. Social Media Links Block: This module provides a simple block for displaying links to your social media profiles. You can configure the block to include icons for your desired social media platforms and customize their appearance and layout.

c. Simple Social Icons: This module allows you to display social media icons with links to your profiles in a block or within your site's content. The module includes a variety of icon sets and customization options for size, color, and alignment.

d. Drupal Social Login: This module enables users to log in or register on your site using their social media accounts, such as Facebook, Google, Twitter, or LinkedIn. The module simplifies the registration process and can improve user retention.

4. Custom Social Media Integration

In some cases, you may need to create a custom module or use external libraries to integrate a specific social media platform with your Drupal site. This can be achieved using Drupal's HTTP client, Guzzle, to make API requests and handle responses. Additionally, Drupal's Plugin API and Services API can be used to create custom plugins and services that interact with social media APIs.

Conclusion

Integrating social media platforms with your Drupal site can provide numerous benefits, including increased visibility, enhanced user engagement, and improved search engine rankings. By leveraging contributed modules, custom modules, and external libraries, you can effectively connect your Drupal site with popular social media platforms like Facebook, Twitter, Instagram, and LinkedIn, creating a more engaging and interactive experience for your users.

11.3. Integrating Drupal with CRM and Marketing Platforms

Customer Relationship Management (CRM) and marketing platforms play a crucial role in managing customer data, optimizing marketing campaigns, and streamlining sales processes. Integrating these platforms with your Drupal site can help improve customer experience, boost conversions, and increase overall business efficiency. In this deep dive, we will discuss the benefits of integrating Drupal with CRM and marketing platforms and provide an overview of common methods and contributed modules for connecting with popular platforms such as Salesforce, HubSpot, and Mailchimp.

1. Benefits of CRM and Marketing Platform Integration

Integrating CRM and marketing platforms with your Drupal site offers numerous advantages, including:

a. Centralized customer data: Consolidate customer data from your Drupal site with your CRM platform, enabling more effective tracking, analysis, and management of customer interactions.

b. Improved lead generation: Automatically capture leads from your Drupal site and add them to your CRM or marketing platform, streamlining your sales and marketing processes.

c. Personalized marketing campaigns: Leverage customer data to create targeted and personalized marketing campaigns, resulting in higher engagement and conversion rates.

d. Enhanced customer experience: Provide a seamless user experience by synchronizing user data between your Drupal site and CRM or marketing platform, enabling personalized content and targeted offers.

2. Common Integration Methods

Several methods can be used to integrate CRM and marketing platforms with your Drupal site, including:

a. Contributed modules: Numerous contributed modules are available for integrating popular CRM and marketing platforms with Drupal. These modules typically offer pre-built API integrations and user-friendly interfaces for configuring and managing the connection.

b. Custom modules: For specific integrations or custom functionality, you may need to create a custom module that interacts with the desired CRM or marketing platform's API. This can be achieved using Drupal's HTTP client, Guzzle, for making API requests and handling responses.

c. External libraries: Some CRM and marketing platforms provide SDKs (Software Development Kits) or libraries to interact with their APIs. These libraries can be included in your custom Drupal modules using Composer, simplifying the integration process.

3. Contributed Modules for CRM and Marketing Platform Integration

Many contributed modules are available for integrating Drupal with popular CRM and marketing platforms. Some notable examples include:

a. Salesforce Suite: This module provides a suite of tools for integrating Drupal with Salesforce, including mapping Drupal entities to Salesforce objects, synchronizing data, and triggering actions based on events in Drupal or Salesforce.

b. HubSpot Integration: This module enables you to integrate Drupal with HubSpot, allowing you to capture and sync leads, track user activity, and embed HubSpot forms and CTAs on your site.

c. Mailchimp: This module facilitates integration between Drupal and Mailchimp, enabling you to manage mailing lists, subscribe users to lists, and send targeted email campaigns.

4. Custom CRM and Marketing Platform Integration

In some cases, you may need to create a custom module to integrate a specific CRM or marketing platform with your Drupal site. This can be achieved using Drupal's HTTP client, Guzzle, to make API requests and handle responses. Additionally, Drupal's Plugin API and Services API can be used to create custom plugins and services that interact with external APIs.

Conclusion

Integrating CRM and marketing platforms with your Drupal site can greatly enhance customer experience, improve lead generation and marketing campaign efficiency, and streamline business processes. By leveraging contributed modules, custom modules, and external libraries, you can effectively connect your Drupal site with popular CRM and marketing platforms such as Salesforce, HubSpot, and Mailchimp, creating a more efficient and data-driven online presence for your business.

11.4. Other Useful Integrations

In addition to CRM and marketing platforms, there are numerous other third-party services that can be integrated with your Drupal site to enhance its functionality, user experience, and overall performance. In this deep dive, we will explore some of these useful integrations, including analytics, file storage, and geolocation services.

1. Analytics and Reporting Integrations

Integrating analytics and reporting services with your Drupal site can provide valuable insights into user behavior, site performance, and other essential metrics. Examples of popular analytics and reporting integrations include:

a. Google Analytics: This module allows you to integrate Drupal with Google Analytics, tracking user behavior and page views, and providing insights into your site's performance.

b. Matomo (formerly Piwik): This module enables you to integrate Drupal with Matomo, an open-source analytics platform that offers in-depth reporting on user behavior, search engine optimization, and more.

2. File Storage Integrations

Integrating your Drupal site with external file storage services can help improve site performance, simplify backups, and reduce hosting costs. Some popular file storage integrations include:

a. Amazon S3: This module enables you to store and retrieve files from Amazon S3, a scalable and cost-effective cloud storage service.

b. Google Cloud Storage: This module allows you to use Google Cloud Storage as a backend for Drupal's file system, providing a scalable and cost-effective storage solution.

3. Geolocation and Mapping Integrations

Integrating geolocation and mapping services with your Drupal site can enable location-based features, such as displaying maps, searching for nearby points of interest, and providing directions. Some popular geolocation and mapping integrations include:

a. Geolocation Field: This module provides a field type for storing geolocation data and integrates with popular mapping services, such as Google Maps and OpenStreetMap, to display interactive maps on your site.

b. Leaflet: This module integrates Drupal with the Leaflet JavaScript library, enabling you to create and display interactive maps using various mapping providers, such as OpenStreetMap, Mapbox, and Google Maps.

4. Payment Gateway Integrations

Integrating payment gateways with your Drupal site can facilitate secure and seamless transactions for your e-commerce store or subscription-based services. Some popular payment gateway integrations include:

a. Commerce Stripe: This module integrates Drupal Commerce with Stripe, a popular payment gateway that supports credit cards, debit cards, and other payment methods.

b. Commerce PayPal: This module enables Drupal Commerce to accept payments through PayPal, a widely used online payment platform.

5. Search Integrations

Integrating external search services with your Drupal site can improve search performance, provide more relevant search results, and offer additional search features. Some popular search integrations include:

a. Search API Solr: This module integrates Drupal with the Apache Solr search platform, providing fast and scalable search capabilities.

b. Elasticsearch Connector: This module enables you to connect Drupal with Elasticsearch, a powerful and scalable search and analytics engine.

Conclusion

Integrating your Drupal site with third-party services can significantly enhance its functionality, user experience, and overall performance. By leveraging contributed modules, custom modules, and external libraries, you can effectively integrate your Drupal site with a wide range of useful services, such as analytics, file storage, geolocation, payment gateways, and search platforms, creating a more robust and feature-rich online presence for your organization.

Chapter 12: Migrating and Upgrading to Drupal 10

Upgrading to Drupal 10 can offer significant improvements in performance, security, and overall site management. Whether you're migrating from a previous version of Drupal or from another content management system (CMS), the process can be complex, yet rewarding. In this chapter, we will discuss an overview of the migration and upgrade process, best practices, and key considerations when transitioning to Drupal 10.

1. Migration vs. Upgrade

It's important to understand the difference between migration and upgrade. An upgrade typically refers to updating from one version of Drupal to another, while migration refers to moving your site's content, configuration, and customizations from a different CMS or Drupal version to Drupal 10. Both processes involve similar steps, but migrations may require additional planning and preparation.

2. Planning the Migration or Upgrade

A well-planned migration or upgrade is crucial for a successful transition to Drupal 10. Key steps in the planning process include:

a. Reviewing existing site architecture: Assess your current site structure, content types, taxonomies, and user roles to determine if any adjustments or optimizations are needed before moving to Drupal 10.

b. Identifying customizations: Make a list of custom modules, themes, and configurations that will need to be updated or replaced during the migration or upgrade.

c. Evaluating contributed modules: Review the contributed modules you're currently using and determine if they are compatible with Drupal 10, require updates, or need to be replaced with alternative modules.

d. Creating a backup and staging environment: Back up your existing site and create a staging environment where you can perform the migration or upgrade without affecting your live site.

3.   Migrating Content and Configuration

Drupal 10 provides built-in migration tools and contributed modules, such as the Migrate API, to facilitate the process of moving your content and configuration to the new platform. This includes importing content types, users, taxonomies, and other site configurations. You may also need to create custom migration scripts for unique content or configuration elements.

4.   Upgrading and Replacing Modules and Themes

During the migration or upgrade process, you will need to update or replace contributed modules and custom themes. This may involve updating module code to ensure compatibility with Drupal 10 or finding alternative modules with similar functionality. Custom themes will need to be updated to work with Drupal 10's theming system and adhere to new best practices.

5.   Testing and Quality Assurance

Thorough testing and quality assurance are critical when migrating or upgrading to Drupal 10. This includes functional testing to ensure all site features are working as expected, performance testing to confirm your site's speed and responsiveness, and security testing to identify any vulnerabilities.

6.   Launching the Drupal 10 Site

Once you've completed the migration or upgrade process, thoroughly tested your site, and addressed any issues, you can launch your Drupal 10 site. This involves switching your domain to point to the new site, monitoring site performance, and addressing any post-launch issues that may arise.

Conclusion

Migrating or upgrading to Drupal 10 can provide numerous benefits for your site, including improved performance, enhanced security, and a more user-friendly content management experience. By carefully planning your migration or upgrade, leveraging Drupal's migration tools, and following best practices for testing and quality assurance, you can successfully transition to Drupal 10 and enjoy the benefits of the latest version of this powerful CMS.

12.1. Planning Your Migration

Planning is a critical step in any migration process. A well-planned migration can help you avoid potential pitfalls, minimize downtime, and ensure a smooth transition to your new Drupal 10 site. In this deep dive, we will cover the essential aspects of planning your migration, including assessing your current site, gathering requirements, creating a timeline, and preparing your team for the migration process.

1. Assessing Your Current Site

Before starting the migration process, it's essential to assess your current site to determine its structure, content, and functionality. This assessment will help you understand the scope of your migration and identify potential challenges. Key aspects of your site to review include:

a. Content types and taxonomies: Review your site's content types and taxonomies to ensure they are organized efficiently and accurately reflect your content structure.

b. Modules and themes: Make a list of all the contributed and custom modules and themes currently in use on your site. This will help you identify which modules need to be updated, replaced, or removed during the migration process.

c. Custom code and integrations: Identify any custom code or third-party integrations that may need to be updated or replaced to ensure compatibility with Drupal 10.

2. Gathering Requirements

As part of the planning process, you'll need to gather requirements for your new Drupal 10 site. This includes understanding the goals of the migration, such as improving site performance, enhancing user experience, or adding new features. You should also consider any new content types, taxonomies, or functionality that you want to implement in your Drupal 10 site.

3. Creating a Migration Timeline

Developing a realistic timeline for your migration is crucial for managing expectations and ensuring that your team has adequate time to complete all necessary tasks. Your timeline should include milestones for each stage of the migration process, such as:

a. Planning and preparation

b. Content and configuration migration

c. Module and theme updates or replacements

d. Testing and quality assurance

e. Site launch and post-launch support

    4.   Preparing Your Team

A successful migration requires a well-prepared team. Ensure that all team members, including developers, designers, content editors, and project managers, understand their roles and responsibilities during the migration process. It's also essential to provide any necessary training on Drupal 10, as well as any new tools or technologies that will be used during the migration.

    5.   Creating a Staging Environment

A staging environment is a replica of your live site that you can use to test the migration process without affecting your production site. Set up a staging environment as part of your planning process to ensure that all migration tasks can be tested and refined before being applied to your live site.

    6.   Backup and Rollback Plan

Backing up your current site is an essential step in the planning process. This ensures that you can quickly restore your site to its previous state if any issues arise during the migration. In addition to creating backups, you should also develop a rollback plan that outlines the steps to be taken if the migration needs to be reversed.

Conclusion

A well-planned migration can help ensure a smooth transition to your new Drupal 10 site. By assessing your current site, gathering requirements, creating a timeline, and preparing your team, you can set the stage for a successful migration. Additionally, setting up a staging environment and developing a backup and rollback plan can provide an extra layer of security, helping you mitigate any risks associated with the migration process.

12.2. Migrating Content, Users, and Configuration

Migrating content, users, and configuration is a crucial aspect of the Drupal migration process. Ensuring that these elements are transferred accurately and efficiently can help you maintain the integrity of your site while minimizing the impact on your users. In this deep dive, we will explore various tools, techniques, and best practices for migrating content, users, and configuration to Drupal 10.

1. Drupal Migrate API

The Migrate API is a powerful built-in tool in Drupal 10 that provides a framework for migrating data from various sources, including older versions of Drupal and other content management systems. Migrate API allows you to define custom migration scripts that define the mapping between source and destination content types, fields, and other configuration elements.

2. Migrate Modules

There are several contributed modules available that can help you streamline the migration process. Some popular migrate modules include:

a. Migrate Drupal: This module provides a set of migration plugins and configuration templates for migrating from older versions of Drupal to Drupal 10.

b. Migrate Plus: Migrate Plus extends the core Migrate API with additional features, such as support for XML and JSON data sources and reusable migration configurations.

c. Migrate Tools: This module provides a set of Drush and Drupal Console commands for managing and executing migration tasks.

3. Migrating Content

To migrate content, you will need to create migration scripts that define the mapping between source and destination content types and fields. This can be done using the Migrate API's YAML configuration files. For complex migrations, you may need to create custom source, process, or destination plugins to handle specific data transformations or content relationships.

4. Migrating Users

User migration involves transferring user accounts, including roles and permissions, from your existing site to Drupal 10. You can use the Migrate API to create user migration scripts that map user data, such as usernames, email addresses, and passwords, to the appropriate fields in Drupal 10. Additionally, you can migrate user roles and permissions by creating migration scripts that map the source roles and permissions to the corresponding roles and permissions in your new site.

5. Migrating Configuration

Configuration migration involves transferring your site's settings, such as content types, taxonomies, views, and display configurations, from your existing site to Drupal 10. The Migrate API can be used to create configuration migration scripts that map source configuration elements to their corresponding Drupal 10 counterparts. In some cases, you may need to create custom migration scripts to handle unique configuration elements or to account for changes in Drupal 10's configuration system.

6. Testing and Validation

Thorough testing and validation are essential for ensuring the accuracy and completeness of your content, user, and configuration migration. After running your migration scripts, review your Drupal 10 site to ensure that all content, users, and configuration elements have been transferred correctly. Check for issues such as missing or incomplete data, broken links, or incorrect display settings. Make any necessary adjustments to your migration scripts and re-run the migration process as needed to address any issues.

Conclusion

Migrating content, users, and configuration is a critical aspect of the Drupal migration process. By leveraging the Migrate API, contributed modules, and custom migration scripts, you can effectively transfer these elements to your new Drupal 10 site. Thorough testing and validation can help ensure that your migration is accurate and complete, setting the stage for a successful transition to Drupal 10.

12.3. Upgrading from Drupal 8 or 9

Upgrading your Drupal site from version 8 or 9 to Drupal 10 can be a seamless process, thanks to the similarities in architecture and the use of the same configuration management system. This deep dive will guide you through the essential steps for a successful upgrade, including updating modules and themes, managing deprecated code, and preparing your site for the new version.

1. Update Modules and Themes

Before upgrading to Drupal 10, it is crucial to ensure that all your contributed modules and themes are compatible with the new version. Check each module's and theme's project page for compatibility information and update them accordingly. If a module or theme is not compatible, look for alternatives or consider custom development to replace the functionality.

2.   Update Custom Code

Custom code, such as modules and themes, should also be reviewed and updated to ensure compatibility with Drupal 10. Utilize tools like the Upgrade Status module and the Drupal-check command-line tool to identify deprecated code and update it according to Drupal 10 standards.

3.   Manage Deprecated Code

Drupal 10 introduces new APIs and deprecates some older ones. Identify deprecated code in your custom modules and themes using the aforementioned tools, and update the code to use the latest APIs. You can refer to Drupal.org's API documentation for guidance on the new APIs and how to update your code.

4.   Prepare Your Site

Before upgrading, ensure that your site is running on the latest minor version of Drupal 8 or 9. Additionally, ensure that your hosting environment meets the system requirements for Drupal 10, such as PHP and database versions. You should also check your site's configuration and ensure that there are no errors or inconsistencies.

5. Backup Your Site

Create a backup of your site's codebase, database, and files before starting the upgrade process. This will allow you to restore your site to its previous state if any issues arise during the upgrade.

6. Upgrade Process

The upgrade process from Drupal 8 or 9 to Drupal 10 is simplified due to the configuration management system and the similarities in architecture. You can use the core update manager or the command-line tools, such as Drush or Drupal Console, to perform the upgrade.

a. Update your site's codebase by replacing the core files with the Drupal 10 core files. Ensure that you keep your custom and contributed modules, themes, and libraries.

b. Update your site's database using the command-line tools or the update manager UI. This will apply any necessary updates to your site's schema and configuration.

c. Test your site thoroughly after the upgrade, checking for any errors, missing functionality, or visual issues. Address any issues and retest until you are satisfied with the upgrade.

7. Post-upgrade Tasks

After the upgrade, perform a thorough review of your site to ensure that all functionality is working as expected. You should also review your site's performance, security, and SEO to ensure that the upgrade has not negatively impacted these areas. Address any issues and monitor your site closely during the initial post-upgrade period.

Conclusion

Upgrading from Drupal 8 or 9 to Drupal 10 is a relatively straightforward process due to the shared architecture and configuration management system. By updating modules, themes, and custom code, preparing your site and environment, and following best practices during the upgrade process, you can ensure a smooth transition to Drupal 10. Don't forget to test your site thoroughly after the upgrade and address any issues to maintain a high-quality user experience.

12.4. Troubleshooting and Post-Migration Tasks

After migrating or upgrading to Drupal 10, it is crucial to address any issues that may arise and perform post-migration tasks to ensure the continued stability, performance, and security of your site. This deep dive will explore common troubleshooting tips, post-migration tasks, and best practices to maintain a successful Drupal 10 site.

1. Troubleshooting Common Issues

Migration and upgrade processes may introduce various issues, ranging from missing content to broken functionality. Below are some common troubleshooting tips:

a. Missing or Incomplete Content: Review your migration scripts and logs to identify any errors or skipped content. Adjust your migration scripts as needed and re-run the migration process to address missing or incomplete content.

b. Broken Functionality: Check for errors in the Drupal log or the browser console to identify any issues with custom or contributed modules and themes. Update or fix the problematic code and clear the cache to resolve the issue.

c. Visual Issues: Review your site's theme and CSS to identify any missing or incorrect styling. Update the theme or CSS as needed to address any visual inconsistencies.

d. Configuration Issues: Check your site's configuration for errors or inconsistencies, and update the configuration as needed to resolve any issues.

2. Post-Migration Tasks

After migration or upgrade, perform the following tasks to ensure the continued stability, performance, and security of your site:

a. Test and Validate: Thoroughly test your site's functionality, performance, and appearance to identify and address any issues that may have been introduced during the migration or upgrade process.

b. Update User Roles and Permissions: Review and update user roles and permissions to ensure that users have the appropriate level of access to the site's content and functionality.

c. Update Content Workflows: Review and update your site's content workflows to align with any changes in content types, fields, or user roles introduced during the migration or upgrade process.

d. Monitor and Optimize Performance: Monitor your site's performance after migration or upgrade and implement performance optimization strategies, such as caching, CDN integration, and image optimization, to ensure optimal user experience.

e. Review and Update SEO: Assess and update your site's SEO settings and metadata to maintain search engine visibility and rankings.

3. Ongoing Maintenance and Best Practices

To maintain a successful Drupal 10 site, follow these ongoing maintenance and best practices:

a. Keep Modules and Themes Up to Date: Regularly update your site's contributed modules and themes to ensure compatibility, stability, and security.

b. Apply Security Updates: Stay informed of any security updates for Drupal core, contributed modules, and themes, and apply these updates promptly to protect your site from potential threats.

c. Regularly Monitor Performance and Security: Continuously monitor your site's performance and security to identify and address any issues before they impact your users.

d. Maintain Regular Backups: Create regular backups of your site's codebase, database, and files to ensure that you can quickly restore your site in the event of data loss or other issues.

Conclusion

Troubleshooting and post-migration tasks are essential for maintaining a successful Drupal 10 site after migrating or upgrading. By addressing common issues, performing post-migration tasks, and following ongoing maintenance and best practices, you can ensure the continued stability, performance, and security of your Drupal 10 site. Regular testing, monitoring, and updates will help you maintain a high-quality user experience and protect your site from potential threats.

Appendix A: Drupal 10 Resources

This appendix provides a list of useful resources for Drupal 10 developers, site builders, and site administrators. These resources cover various topics, including documentation, tutorials, support forums, and contributed modules and themes. Familiarizing yourself with these resources will help you get the most out of Drupal 10 and ensure a successful experience.

1. Official Drupal Resources

a. Drupal.org: The official Drupal website provides comprehensive documentation, community-contributed modules and themes, and support forums. Visit https://www.drupal.org/ for more information.

b. Drupal 10 User Guide: The official Drupal 10 User Guide offers step-by-step instructions and best practices for building and managing Drupal sites. Visit https://www.drupal.org/docs/user_guide/en/index.html for the complete guide.

c. Drupal API Reference: The Drupal API reference provides detailed information on Drupal core APIs and functions. Visit https://api.drupal.org/ for the complete API reference.

2. Tutorials and Blogs

a. Drupalize.Me: Drupalize.Me offers high-quality video tutorials and written guides covering a wide range of Drupal topics. Visit https://drupalize.me/ for their extensive library.

b. Lullabot: Lullabot provides insightful articles and tutorials on Drupal development, theming, and site building. Visit https://www.lullabot.com/articles for their latest content.

c. Acquia Developer Center: Acquia's Developer Center provides articles, tutorials, and webinars on Drupal development, site building, and hosting. Visit https://dev.acquia.com/ for more information.

3. Support Forums and Community

a. Drupal.org Forums: The official Drupal forums provide a platform for users to ask questions, share knowledge, and discuss various Drupal-related topics. Visit https://www.drupal.org/forum for more information.

b. Drupal Stack Exchange: The Drupal Stack Exchange is a question and answer platform for Drupal developers and administrators. Visit https://drupal.stackexchange.com/ to ask questions or find answers.

c. Drupal Groups: Drupal Groups provide a space for users to connect, collaborate, and discuss specific topics related to Drupal. Visit https://groups.drupal.org/ to find a group that interests you.

4. Contributed Modules and Themes

a. Drupal.org Project Repository: The official Drupal project repository provides an extensive collection of community-contributed modules and themes for Drupal 10. Visit https://www.drupal.org/project/project_module and https://www.drupal.org/project/project_theme to browse the available modules and themes.

b. Drupal Module Finder: The Drupal Module Finder helps you discover and compare contributed modules by filtering based on category, popularity, and more. Visit https://www.drupalmodules.com/ for more information.

    5.   Drupal Events and Conferences

a. DrupalCon: DrupalCon is the largest annual Drupal conference, bringing together developers, site builders, and users from around the world. Visit https://events.drupal.org/ for more information on upcoming DrupalCon events.

b. DrupalCamps: DrupalCamps are regional events that offer sessions, workshops, and networking opportunities for the local Drupal community. Visit https://www.drupical.com/ to find a DrupalCamp near you.

    6.   Miscellaneous Resources

a. Drush: Drush is a command-line shell and scripting interface for Drupal, providing a powerful set of tools for managing your site. Visit https://www.drush.org/ for more information.

b. Drupal Console: The Drupal Console is a suite of command-line tools for Drupal site development and management. Visit https://drupalconsole.com/ to learn more.

By utilizing these resources, you can expand your knowledge, solve problems, and connect with the Drupal community. Stay up-to-date with the latest developments and best

Appendix B: Drupal Terminology Glossary

This glossary provides definitions for common Drupal terms and concepts. Familiarizing yourself with this terminology will help you better understand Drupal's architecture and functionality.

1. Block: A reusable piece of content or functionality that can be placed in various regions within a Drupal site's layout.
2. Content type: A pre-defined structure for content, consisting of fields and display settings, that determines how the content is stored and displayed.
3. Core: The base Drupal installation, which includes essential features and APIs for building and managing a Drupal site.
4. Distribution: A pre-packaged version of Drupal, including core, contributed modules, and configurations, tailored for a specific purpose or industry.
5. Entity: A unit of content or configuration in Drupal, such as nodes, users, taxonomy terms, or blocks.
6. Field: A piece of data associated with an entity, such as a title, body text, image, or date.
7. Hook: A way for modules to interact with and alter Drupal's core functionality or other modules' functionality.

8. Module: A package of PHP, JavaScript, and/or CSS files that extends Drupal's functionality or adds new features.

9. Node: A piece of content created within a Drupal site, such as an article, page, or blog post.

10. Region: A defined area within a Drupal site's layout where blocks can be placed.

11. Taxonomy: A system for categorizing content in Drupal using terms organized within vocabularies.

12. Theme: A collection of files that define the look and feel of a Drupal site, including HTML, CSS, JavaScript, and template files.

13. View: A dynamic, database-driven display of content on a Drupal site, created using the Views module.

14. Views: A powerful contributed module for creating, managing, and displaying dynamic lists of content in Drupal.

15. Vocabulary: A group of taxonomy terms used to categorize content in Drupal.

Understanding these terms will help you navigate Drupal's documentation, community discussions, and development process more effectively. As you continue to work with Drupal, you'll likely encounter additional terminology specific to your projects or use cases. Don't hesitate to seek clarification or consult additional resources to expand your Drupal vocabulary.

Appendix C: Module and Theme Development Resources

This appendix provides a list of resources to help you get started with module and theme development in Drupal 10. Familiarizing yourself with these resources will help you learn best practices, find example code, and ensure a successful development experience.

1. Official Drupal Resources

a. Drupal.org Documentation: Drupal.org provides extensive documentation on creating custom modules and themes. Visit https://www.drupal.org/docs/creating-custom-modules and https://www.drupal.org/docs/theming-drupal for detailed guides.

b. Drupal API Reference: The Drupal API reference provides detailed information on Drupal core APIs and functions, which are essential for module and theme development. Visit https://api.drupal.org/ for the complete API reference.

c. Drupal.org Project Repository: The official Drupal project repository provides a wealth of community-contributed modules and themes, which can serve as examples and inspiration for your projects. Visit https://www.drupal.org/project/project_module and https://www.drupal.org/project/project_theme to browse the available modules and themes.

   2. Tutorials and Blogs

a. Drupalize.Me: Drupalize.Me offers high-quality video tutorials and written guides covering various aspects of Drupal module and theme development. Visit https://drupalize.me/ for their extensive library.

b. Lullabot: Lullabot provides insightful articles and tutorials on Drupal development, theming, and site building. Visit https://www.lullabot.com/articles for their latest content.

c. OSTraining: OSTraining offers a range of video tutorials and articles on Drupal module and theme development. Visit https://www.ostraining.com/ for more information.

   3. Tools and Libraries

a. Drush: Drush is a command-line shell and scripting interface for Drupal, providing a powerful set of tools for module and theme development. Visit https://www.drush.org/ for more information.

b. Drupal Console: The Drupal Console is a suite of command-line tools for Drupal site development and management. Visit https://drupalconsole.com/ to learn more.

c. Composer: Composer is a dependency manager for PHP that is widely used in Drupal projects. Visit https://getcomposer.org/ for more information.

d. Git: Git is a version control system used for managing Drupal codebases, including contributed modules and themes. Visit https://git-scm.com/ for more information.

4. Drupal Events and Conferences

a. DrupalCon: DrupalCon is the largest annual Drupal conference, offering sessions, workshops, and networking opportunities for developers, site builders, and users. Visit https://events.drupal.org/ for more information on upcoming DrupalCon events.

b. DrupalCamps: DrupalCamps are regional events that offer sessions, workshops, and networking opportunities for the local

Drupal community. Visit https://www.drupical.com/ to find a DrupalCamp near you.

5. Support Forums and Community

a. Drupal.org Forums: The official Drupal forums provide a platform for users to ask questions, share knowledge, and discuss module and theme development topics. Visit https://www.drupal.org/forum for more information.

b. Drupal Stack Exchange: The Drupal Stack Exchange is a question and answer platform for Drupal developers and administrators. Visit https://drupal.stackexchange.com/ to ask questions or find answers.

c. Drupal Groups: Drupal Groups provide a space for users to connect, collaborate, and discuss specific topics related to Drupal, including module and theme development. Visit https://groups.drupal.org/ to find a group that interests you.

By utilizing these resources, you can expand your knowledge, find inspiration, and connect with the Drupal community. Stay up-to-date with the latest developments and best practices in module and theme development to ensure your projects are successful and maintainable

About the author

Victor Wickström, born in Halmstad, Sweden, has been a passionate web developer since 1994, a time when the landscape of web development was drastically different from what it is today. Back then, the lack of sophisticated Integrated Development Environments (IDEs) proved to be a challenge, but Victor, along with a close friend, stepped up to create their own IDE to streamline their work.

In 2010, while living in Örebro, Victor discovered Drupal and quickly embraced the platform as a powerful content management system for web development. At the time, he was employed by Impera Kommunikation, where he began integrating Drupal into his work. Later, Victor moved to Stockholm and eventually settled in Copenhagen, Denmark, where he has been living for the past 10 years.

Over the past 11 years, Victor has been a dedicated Drupal developer and has made contributions to the Drupal community. In his current role at Awave, Victor serves as a Drupal developer, bringing his extensive experience and passion for web development to the customers. Through his expertise and commitment, he continues to drive the success of numerous Drupal projects and helps clients bring their visions to life on the web.

If you have any suggestions, questions, or would like to get in touch with Victor, he can be reached at his email: victor.wickstrom@gmail.com.